At Issue

Are Graphic Music Lyrics Harmful?

Other Books in the At Issue Series:

At Issue

Are Graphic Music Lyrics Harmful?

Noah Berlatsky, Book Editor

GREENHAVEN PRESS
A part of Gale, Cengage Learning

Farmington Hills, Mich • San Francisco • New York • Waterville, Maine
Meriden, Conn • Mason, Ohio • Chicago

GALE
CENGAGE Learning™

Judy Galens, *Manager, Frontlist Acquisitions*

© 2016 Greenhaven Press, a part of Gale, Cengage Learning.

Gale and Greenhaven Press are registered trademarks used herein under license.

For more information, contact:
Greenhaven Press
27500 Drake Rd.
Farmington Hills, MI 48331-3535
Or you can visit our Internet site at gale.cengage.com

For product information and technology assistance, contact us at

Gale Customer Support, 1-800-877-4253
For permission to use material from this text or product, submit all requests online at www.cengage.com/permissions

Further permissions questions can be e-mailed to permissionrequest@cengage.com

Articles in Greenhaven Press anthologies are often edited for length to meet page requirements. In addition, original titles of these works are changed to clearly present the main thesis and to explicitly indicate the author's opinion. Every effort is made to ensure that Greenhaven Press accurately reflects the original intent of the authors. Every effort has been made to trace the owners of copyrighted material.

Cover image © Images.com/Corbis.

LIBRARY OF CONGRESS CATALOGING-IN-PUBLICATION DATA

Are graphic music lyrics harmful? / Noah Berlatsky, book editor.
    pages cm. -- (At issue)
Includes bibliographical references and index.
ISBN 978-0-7377-7376-7 (hardcover) -- ISBN 978-0-7377-7377-4 (pbk.)
1. Popular music--Moral and ethical aspects. 2. Popular music--Social aspects. I. Berlatsky, Noah, editor.
ML3918.P67A88 2016
363.4--dc23
                          2015029174

Printed in the United States of America
  1 2 3 4 5   20 19 18 17 16

Contents

Introduction

One of the most controversial performers in recent music is Miley Cyrus. Cyrus began her career as a mostly wholesome teen pop icon, appearing as Hannah Montana in the show of the same name on the Disney Channel. In 2013, however, she moved toward a more sexual style. Her performance at the 2013 MTV Video Music Awards (VMA) became instantly infamous. She danced with teddy bears, wore a bikini that matched her flesh tone, stuck her tongue out lewdly, groped one of her back up dancers, and mimed sex with R&B performer Robin Thicke.

Many commentators have argued that Cyrus's sexualization is harmful. For example, Dionne Taylor, an academic and expert in criminal law, studied black women aged fifteen to twenty-nine in Birmingham and London and concluded that many young girls see sexualization as "part and parcel" of their everyday lives. Taylor argued that "the explicit dance moves and foul-mouthed lyrics fuel negative attitudes towards women and affect women's confidence, education and even their employment prospects."[1]

Some parents were particularly upset because Cyrus had originally appealed to a very young fan base. Kelly Wallace for CNN reported a number of disappointed and angry comments from parents she talked to or who posted on the CNN Facebook page. "It's a damn shame that Miley is doing this to herself, making a vulgar joke out of her talents and her beauty, but it's a much bigger shame that she's doing it to her young fans and other young people (who) see her in the media," one mother of teenaged boys said. Another commented, "I just

---

1. Quoted in Laura Cox, "Raunchy, Hyper-Sexualised Popstars Like Miley Cyrus and Rihanna Damage Girls' Self-Esteem—and Could Harm Education and Job Prospects—Says Leading Academic," *Daily Mail*, September 13, 2013. http://www.dailymail.co.uk/femail/article-2419993/Miley-Cyrus-Rihanna-damage-girls-self-esteem--harm-education-job-prospects--says-academic.html.

find it extremely discouraging and difficult to hold out hope for the improved status of women in this world when even the most entitled among us so negatively reinforce the worst stereotypes and misogynistic attitudes about women."[2]

Other pundits, however, have argued that Cyrus's performances are empowering and feminist. Jincey Lumpkin, a writer for *The Huffington Post*, said, "I am sick and tired of people assigning a negative personal value judgment to individuals who choose to express themselves sexually." Lumpkin maintains that Cyrus is appropriating the crotch-grabbing, aggressive sexuality of male pop performers, a move that Lumpkin sees as liberating and transgressive.[3]

Richard Fry, also on *Huffington Post*, added that he thought Cyrus's VMA performance was "brilliant, funny and confident." He added that Cyrus was doing exactly what other teen stars like Britney Spears and Christina Aguilera had done—moving on from their teen career by embracing adult sexuality. He points out that when Cyrus "pushes the over-sized finger of a foam hand between her legs and thrusts it out to a cheering crowd," she is showing that she is more of a man than Robin Thicke, with whom she's dancing. Fry sees her as in control and "having fun," which is "exactly what a proper pop star should be doing." All the controversy, he adds, only helps promote her and ensures that her "next performance will be even more sensational."[4]

A number of critics took issue not with Cyrus's sexuality but with her approach to race. During her performance, Cyrus shook her rear in a dance style known as twerking, which had

2. Quoted in Kelly Wallace, "Would You Take Kids to See Miley?," CNN, February 25, 2014. http://www.cnn.com/2013/08/27/living/outraged-parents-why-miley-cyrus-performance-sets-girls-and-women-back.

3. Jincey Lumpkin, "Why Miley Cyrus Is a Feminist Icon," *Huffington Post*, October 14, 2013. http://www.huffingtonpost.com/jincey-lumpkin/why-miley-cyrus-is-a-feminist-icon_b_4078373.html.

4. Richard Fry, "In Praise of Miley's VMA Performance," *Huffington Post*, August 26, 2013. http://www.huffingtonpost.co.uk/richard-fry/miley-cyrus-vmas_b_3818588.html.

originally been developed by African American performers. Miley also performed with black background singers, one of whom she groped.

Tricia Rose, a professor of Africana studies at Brown University, argues that Cyrus uses racial stereotypes of black people as a way to make herself seem dangerous and adult. "The whole thing struck me as a high school disposition or attitude," she noted, "that way of dressing up in what they think are transgressive ways, this idea that blackness equals transgression."[5] Sociologist Tressie McMillan Cottom points out that the black dancers in the VMA performance were mostly not slender pop stars like Beyoncé and Rihanna, but larger women, like Cottom herself. To have these black women serve as background decoration, Cottom says, shows how the culture treats "bodies like mine as inferior, non-threatening spaces where white women can play at being 'dirty' without risking her sexual appeal."[6]

Another person who felt that Cyrus used background dancers as props was one of the background dancers herself. Hollis Jane, a little person, danced in a teddy bear outfit during Cyrus's VMA performance. Jane said that, "[For the] first time . . . I was being used because of my height, not because of my talent. And I will be the first one to tell you that standing on that stage, in that costume was one of the most degrading things I felt like I could ever do."[7] Jane said the performance seemed designed to encourage the audience to gawk at the little people, and that Cyrus made herself look cool and edgy by presenting those she performed with as freakish or abnormal.

5. Quoted in Daniel D'Addario, "Is Miley Cyrus' Twerking Racist?," *Salon*, June 24, 2013. http://www.salon.com/2013/06/24/is_miley_cyrus_twerking_racist.
6. Tressie McMillan Cottom, "When Your (Brown) Body Is a (White) Wonderland," *tressiemc* (blog), August 27, 2013. http://tressiemc.com/2013/08/27/when-your-brown-body-is-a-white-wonderland.
7. Quoted in Antonia Blumberg, "Miley Cyrus Backup Dancer, Hollis Jane, Speaks Out Against 'Degrading' VMA Performance," *Huffington Post*, October 11, 2013. http://www.huffingtonpost.com/2013/10/11/miley-cyrus-backup-dancer_n_4085057.html.

The viewpoints in this book, *At Issue: Are Graphic Music Lyrics Harmful?*, examine in greater depth many of the issues raised by Miley Cyrus and her music, including sexualization and racism in music. The authors also address additional topics, such as the relationship between music and violence.

1

Intent Is a Flawed Standard for Determining Legitimate Threats

Jessica Mason Pieklo

Jessica Mason Pieklo is a writer and adjunct law professor in Minneapolis/St. Paul, Minnesota. She is the former assistant director of the Health Law Clinic at Hamline Law School.

The Supreme Court heard a case dealing with Anthony Elonis, a man who posted rap lyrics online, referencing his ex-wife, who saw the lyrics as threats. The legal question at issue is whether speech should be seen as a true threat based on the intent of the speaker or on the interpretation of a reasonable listener. The law needs to evolve and find a way to hold people accountable for violent speech, especially considering the nature of online threats. However, given the fact that justices tend to be white and male and unaccustomed to facing power disparities themselves, it seems unlikely that the law will deal with these cases appropriately.

In the age of GamerGate, targeted online abuse of women of color, and increased attempts by the conservative right to weaponize the First Amendment to their advantage, the *Elonis* case currently before the Supreme Court perfectly captures the limits of our legal system. Namely, we must adapt the law to our rapidly changing digital communications landscape while avoiding the criminalization of speech or privileging some speakers over others. The problem is, I don't know if that's possible.

Eminem and True Threats

Those limits were on display Monday [December 1, 2014] as the Roberts Court [that is, the Supreme Court under John Roberts] wrestled over when violent online speech constitutes a criminal "true threat," and when such speech should be constitutionally protected. The case involves Anthony Elonis, a Pennsylvania man convicted in 2010 under federal law for posting a series of violent and threatening messages on his Facebook page. Elonis reportedly began making public statements on the social media site shortly after his wife and their two small children moved out. Elonis also began acting out at his then workplace, including engaging in behavior that led to a co-worker filing five sexual harassment complaints against him.

This chasm between what constitutes free speech and what constitutes criminal threats is one federal courts have struggled with in recent years.

After he was eventually fired, Elonis' posts became increasingly violent and targeted. According to court documents, Elonis' Facebook statements included threats to kill his ex-wife, blow up the sheriff's office, shoot up a kindergarten, and attack former co-workers. Elonis' ex-wife testified that she was "extremely afraid" and felt like she was being stalked by Elonis' posts. Elonis was eventually charged and convicted under a federal statute that makes it a crime to "transmit in interstate or foreign commerce any communication containing any threat to kidnap any person or any threat to injure the person of another." Elonis challenged the conviction, arguing that his Facebook posts were not criminal threats, but merely creative expressions and therefore protected by the First Amendment.

Elonis' attorneys claim that Elonis did not intend for his statements to be actual threats; they say he was just imitating Eminem. But the federal government maintains that the speaker's motivation is not how the Court should determine the standard for what constitutes a "threat." Under the argument put forward by the federal government, if a "reasonable person" would interpret an Internet rant as a threat, that should be enough to remove any First Amendment protections from that speech.

No Middle Ground

This chasm between what constitutes free speech and what constitutes criminal threats is one federal courts have struggled with in recent years, especially after 2003, when the Supreme Court ruled in *Virginia v. Black* that burning a cross could sometimes count as free speech. On Monday, the Court sought to fill the divide between whether a threat can be determined by the speaker or the recipient with some middle ground. But in the case of violent online messages, middle ground may be an impossibility—no matter how hard the justices search for it.

For example, during Monday's arguments, Chief Justice John Roberts emphasized the context of the speech at issue, offering up teenage speakers as an example of how and why the framing of the violent messages matter. "You don't take what is on the Internet in the abstract and say, 'This person wants to do something horrible,'" said Roberts, speaking about how courts in the future might consider controversial speech in that hypothetical middle ground framework. "You are familiar with the context."

Elonis' attorney pointed out that in order to understand the context of the speech at issue, courts must consider the speaker's intent—which would mean adopting the standard Elonis was advocating.

The chief justice returned to this theme of context with the federal government's proposed "reasonable person" standard, asking Deputy Solicitor General Michael Dreeben, "If you have a statement made in the style of rap music . . . is the reasonable person supposed to be someone familiar with that style and the use of what might be viewed as threatening words in connection with that music?"

Dreeben responded that of course it depends whom the speaker is speaking to. That's why, he said, Elonis' case was different than the government trying to prosecute entertainers like Eminem, who threaten women with rape and murder daily in the name of art.

What you don't have perfect freedom to do is to make statements that are like the ones in this case.

The chief justice didn't appear that convinced, quoting the lyrics from Eminem's "'97 Bonnie and Clyde," which Elonis' attorney claimed had in part inspired his client to take to Facebook for his rants. "What about the language at pages 54 to 55 of the Petitioner's brief?" asked Roberts. "You know, 'Dada make a nice bed for Mommy at the bottom of the lake,' . . . this is during the context of a domestic dispute between a husband and wife. 'There goes Mama splashing in the water, no more fighting with Dad,' you know, all that stuff."

Dreeben responded that Eminem had been trying to broadly entertain an audience. Elonis, on the other hand, had a specific history with the targets of his threatening posts.

But Roberts didn't appear to be swayed, suggesting the government's proposed standard would leave rappers-in-training everywhere having to preemptively declare their artistic intent in order to be protected from possible prosecution. "So how do you start out if you want to be a rap artist?" he asked. "Your first communication you can't say, I'm an artist, right?"

"I think that you have perfect freedom to engage in rap artistry," responded Dreeben. Again, he reiterated that Elonis' wife, considering the background of the situation, could have reasonably concluded that his threats were legitimate. "What you don't have perfect freedom to do is to make statements that are like the ones in this case, after the individual receives a protection from abuse order from a court which was based on Facebook posts that his wife took as threatening, he comes out with a post and says, 'Fold up that PFA [protection from abuse] and put it in your pocket: Will it stop a bullet?' He knows that his wife is reading these posts," he continued.

Getting Away with Threats

Elonis' attorney closed with a dire warning for the justices that should they adopt the standard argued by the federal government it would be akin to imposing five years of felony liability anytime a listener is confused by the intention of a speaker. According to Elonis' attorney, his client's attempting to craft rap lyrics wasn't a "recent invention," and noted that Elonis' postings included "long and painful-to-read rap which has nothing to do with his wife."

"Again, you can imagine a situation where somebody says, 'I'm posting this for entertainment purposes only,'" Elonis said, referring to the posts.

In the end it was Justice Samuel Alito, of all people, who seemed to grasp the real danger to women lurking in the *Elonis* case. "Well, this sounds like a road map for threatening a spouse and getting away with it," he said. "You put it in rhyme and you put some stuff about the Internet on it and you say, 'I'm an aspiring rap artist.'"

At the close of the arguments, though, it appeared as if a majority of the justices were uncomfortable with the government's position that a speaker could be found to have made a criminal threat, so long as a reasonable person would view them as likely to cause fear of harm.

Any sort of "reasonable person" standard, as argued by the federal government, is from the start a legal fiction that will replicate the very inequities it was supposed to counteract.

On the one hand, I'm sympathetic to the First Amendment purists' argument that the answer to bad speech like Elonis' is not to criminalize that speech, but to answer it with more speech. Furthermore, I am definitely reluctant to grant law enforcement any more police power than it already has. So I can see where Elonis' attorneys are coming from. However, it is undeniable that not all online threats and speakers are the same. Women, and especially women of color, face a much more threatening and hostile landscape online, with law enforcement and the private sector often slow to respond. The idea that the "solution" here to online threats would be to put the onus on those harassed individuals to talk back to their abusers and create "more speech" seems to ignore the very reality of power dynamics informing abusive language. And this leaves the courts not much room but to take abusers at their word that no matter how awful and violent the message, it's OK, because they didn't really mean it.

Rights of Speakers vs. Rights of Listeners

If a majority of justices do side with Elonis, such a ruling could have far-reaching consequences, especially in the fight to protect abortion access. The Tenth Circuit Court of Appeals is currently considering arguments from extreme anti-abortion advocate Angel Dillard that her letter promising explosives under the car of Kansas abortion provider Dr. Mila Means did not violate the Freedom of Access to Clinic Entrances (FACE) Act because it wasn't a "true threat." Then there's the case of Mark Holick, a pastor who argues that his "Wanted"-style poster featuring the picture and home address of a Wichita abortion clinic operator is also protected speech.

If a notorious anti-abortion radical like Angel Dillard can defend her actions by claiming that she didn't *mean* them, or if a former partner can posts threats describing in detail the violence he plans to commit without consequence by deeming them "lyrics," how does that protect advocates? That outcome, like we witnessed this summer in the *McCullen v. Coakley* buffer zone case, is a full embrace of the rights of speakers over the rights of listeners. What about my right to be left alone—or abortion providers' rights, or an ex-wife's rights?

That said, I also think the law is so immersed in rape culture and racial inequity that any sort of "reasonable person" standard, as argued by the federal government, is from the start a legal fiction that will replicate the very inequities it was supposed to counteract. If a majority of our federal judges are white men, who do we think is their default "reasonable person"? A Black woman? Not likely. And how does the lack of judicial diversity and a culture steeped in rape apology change the way those judges view the "reasonableness" of a particular threat? Those are vital, difficult issues that so far none of the proposed arguments or standards, in my opinion, adequately address.

The very fact that so many big and important questions won't get answered no matter how the Court rules in *Elonis* is probably the best indication we have of the limits of the courts in their ability to strike any true balance of rights at all. Maybe the major lesson we can take from cases like *Elonis* is that no matter the standard the Court adopts in judging free speech from criminal speech, the outcome always seems to benefit those with the most power. Or, in this case, the loudest voice.

2

Violent Lyrics Increase Aggression

Diana Zuckerman

Diana Zuckerman is the president of the National Center for Health Research and the Cancer Prevention and Treatment Fund.

A study found that college students who listened to metal and rap songs with violent lyrics had an increase in violent thoughts over the short term. The study found little long-term increase in hostility, and no increase in arousal. The study compared different songs by the same artists without violent lyrics as a control, indicating that the increase in aggressiveness was due to lyrical content specifically. Researchers did not look at whether repeated exposure to the same lyrics had a cumulative effect on aggressiveness.

Although rappers have attracted a great deal of attention for violent song lyrics, most of the public attention about the impact of media violence on youth has been on movies, TV and videogames. Since kids often listen to music while doing other activities, it is possible that violent lyrics are not as influential as visual media.

Lyrics and Aggressive Thoughts

On the other hand, favorite songs may be listened to hundreds of times, and can have a strong emotional impact. For those reasons, violent songs could be more influential than other media violence.

Previous studies have found that enjoying or listening to heavy metal and rap music correlates with hostile attitudes, negative attitudes toward women, lower academic performance, behavior problems in school, drug use and arrests. Experimental studies of music without lyrics found that listening to "tense" music resulted in people writing more unpleasant stories in the Thematic Apperception Test.

A new study of violent lyrics is based on five experiments, each conducted on students from a large Midwestern university. Each study ranged in size between 60 and 160 students, approximately half male and half female.

Students who listened to the violent song expressed more hostility and aggressive thoughts immediately afterwards.

In each experiment, young people listened to the lyrics of a song, then completed a scale aimed at measuring whether they were feeling hostile or having aggressive thoughts. Some songs had violent lyrics and some did not; some songs were humorous and others were not.

Hostile feelings and aggressive thoughts were measured in several ways, such as the students' greater tendency to turn incomplete words into hostile words (changing "h_t" to hit rather than hat), and the authors' State Hostility Scale, which consists of 35 sentences describing current feelings, either hostile or friendly (such as "I feel furious" or "I feel like yelling at someone").

Students who listened to the violent song expressed more hostility and aggressive thoughts immediately afterwards. There was no effect of violent lyrics on arousal, understandability of lyrics or familiarity with the songs. However, in some cases if the students had another task between the time they listened to the songs and filled out the questionnaires, they did not seem more hostile in their responses to the questionnaires, although they continued to have more aggressive thoughts. The students who listened to a violent humorous song were not as influenced as those who listened to a violent song that was not humorous. The authors conclude that humor partially canceled out the effect of violence on state hostility, but did not completely cancel out violence for aggressive cognitions.

Using a meta-analysis on the five experiments, the researchers concluded that violent lyrics increased the students' feelings of hostility and likelihood of interpreting ambiguous cues as hostile, and this was true (although less influential) even if the violent lyrics were in a humorous song.

The researchers were surprised to find that students who were initially more hostile did not respond differently to the violent songs than those who were less hostile.

Short-Lived Impact

The strength of the studies are that they used songs with similar styles and the same artists, so that the only difference was whether lyrics were violent. They also studied whether the songs increase arousal, not aggressiveness. Surprisingly, they found no differences in arousal by violent songs.

Overall, the findings from the five experiments were consistent with each other, suggesting that listening to even one violent song can have a short-term impact on a college student. But the fact that students did not show increased hostility when they were given another task between listening to the song and participating in the hostility survey or word tasks indicates that the impact of these songs on hostile feelings may be short-lived. However, their impact on aggressive thoughts may be longer lasting.

Because other youth were not studied, it is not possible to know if younger or older students, or less educated youth, would be affected the same way.

Unfortunately, this study does not study the impact of repeated exposure to the same violent lyrics. It seems logical that if the song had an impact after listening just once, the impact would be greater if the student listened to it many times. Because listening just once causes short-term hostility and increases the chances of interpreting ambiguous cues as hostile, the authors note that it is possible that those hostile feelings could generate negative reactions from other people, which could start a cycle of hostile or aggressive behaviors. That, however, was not evaluated in this study.

3

The Media Overhypes the Effects of Violent Music Lyrics

Drew Tewksbury

Drew Tewksbury writes for Los Angeles *magazine and is the managing editor and producer of KCET-TV's* Artbound *transmedia project.*

Following violent incidents, the media often blames violent music, especially metal music. For example, following the shooting of US representative Gabrielle Giffords, the shooter's violence was linked to the fact that he was a fan of metal band Drowning Pool. After the Columbine High School shootings in 1999, the violence was blamed on the fact that the killers listened to the music of Marilyn Manson. There is no evidence that listening to metal music actually caused these violent actions. Blaming violence on music is easy, sensational, and irresponsible.

Whenever a horrific tragedy like the mass killing (and attempted political assassination [of US representative Gabrielle Giffords]) in Tucson takes place, the media often tries to make sense out of such a senseless act. They look to fragments of killer's social life to try explain what drove that person over the edge.

And just as often, the media blames Metal music.

Blaming Metal

Since one of Tucson killer Jared Loughner's favorited videos on YouTube was someone burning an American flag to the tune of Drowning Pool's "Bodies Hit the Floor," the *Washington Post* has turned to metal as a scapegoat. The band released a statement via their website to defend themselves: "We were devastated to learn of the tragic events that occurred in Arizona and that our music has been misinterpreted, again."

The band's song has found controversy before because of a 2003 murder where a teenager killed his parents while listening to the song. The song was also banned from Clear Channel's radio playlist after September 11th. On Tuesday, they issued another statement decrying the WaPo article: "Listening to Drowning Pool music does not make you a bad person. Misleading people does."

Norwegian black metal has been blamed for much violence in Norway, including multiple church burnings.

But for years, music that some consider extreme (Drowning Pool, Judas Priest, Marilyn Manson) and even some decidedly tamer stuff (The Beatles?) has been scapegoated by politicians as the cause for violence.

Here are the Six Most Idiotic Attempts to Blame Musicians for Violent Events:

6. Mayhem & Norwegian Black Metal Violence

Norwegian black metal has been blamed for much violence in Norway, including multiple church burnings. But few black metal bands are more infamous than Mayhem. In 1991, their lead singer Per Yngve Ohlin aka Dead, killed himself in a house owned by the band. Band member Euronymous found the body and went to the store and bought a camera and took pictures of the body, which ended up as album art on one of the bands bootlegs. Rumor has it that pieces of his skull were kept as mementos. Then in 1993, temporary Mayhem member Varg Vikernes (of Burzum) stabbed and killed Euronymous.

Black Metal became subject of intense scrutiny as waves of violence across the country brought the underground music to the media's attention.

5. The Beatles' "Helter Skelter" & Manson Family Murders

Charles Manson predicted that a widespread race war would trigger an end-of-days scenario that he called Helter Skelter. He took the name from a Beatles song off of *The White Album*, which he thought confirmed his notions about the race war apocalypse. The song itself was about a English roller coaster, but former Manson Family member Catherine Share explained his view in a 2009 documentary, *Manson*. "Every single song on the White Album, he felt that they were singing about us. The song 'Helter Skelter'—he was interpreting that to mean the blacks were gonna go up and the whites were gonna go down."

4. Ozzy Osbourne's "Suicide Solution" & Teen Suicide

In the late 1980's Ozzy Osbourne's song "Suicide Solution," faced both media and legal wrath. On January 13, 1986 California youth John McCollum committed suicide while listening to the song. His parents took Osbourne to court, alleging that the song's lyrics caused their son to commit suicide.

Osbourne was cleared.

Judas Priest to Marilyn Manson

3. Judas Priest's "Better by You, Better Than Me" & Suicide Pact

In one of the more famous instances of music as scapegoat, Judas Priest came under scrutiny in 1985 when 18-year-old Raymond Belknap and 20-year-old James Vance shot themselves in the head after drinking, smoking and listening to Judas Priest's album *Stained Glass*. Belknap died and Vance lived for three more years totally disfigured. Their families took Priest to court for a $6.2 million lawsuit, claiming that Priest's song, "Better by You, Better Than Me" contained subliminal messaging. The band was found not guilty, but the case set the precedent for bands to be sued for lyrical content.

2. AC/DC's "Night Prowler" & Serial Killer Richard Ramirez

Serial killer Richard "Night Stalker" Ramirez wreaked havoc on California for 14 months in the 1980s. He committed 16 killings across the state but when he accidentally left an AC/DC hat at one of the crime scenes, the media looked to metal as his motivation for violence. When he was caught and put on trial, Ramirez claimed that AC/DC's song "Night Prowler" inspired him to sneak into people's houses and kill them. The song is actually about a kid sneaking into his girlfriend's house while her parents slept.

And the most messed up attempt to blame a sorta-clownish performer for the actions of some messed up alleged fans is . . .

1. Marilyn Manson & Columbine's killers

When Eric Harris and Dylan Klebold killed 12 students during a rampage at Columbine high school in 1999, the media blamed their "gothness" as having an influence on their atrocious acts. The teens listened to industrial act KMFDM, German metal-heads Rammstein, and Marylin Manson. Manson received the brunt of the blame, and took to his own defense by writing an eloquent essay for *Rolling Stone* and appearing in Michael Moore's documentary *Bowling for Columbine*. When Moore asked Manson what he would have said to them just moments before the massacre, Manson replied, "I wouldn't say a thing. I would just listen to them . . . and that's what nobody did."

4

Rap Music Can Both Encourage and Discourage Violence

Peak Johnson

Peak Johnson is a founder and editor of the teen community newspaper The North Philly Metropolis *and writes for a number of publications.*

In Philadelphia, local rap groups often include violent content in their lyrics. To some degree, this is a reflection of life in poor black communities in Philadelphia, which can be violent and difficult. But there is also a concern that the music glorifies the violence or may lead people to see violence as an acceptable option. At the same time, hip-hop groups often include positive messages in their songs, and many are involved in antiviolence efforts. So the relationship between music lyrics and violence is complicated and individual; it may discourage violence in some ways and encourage it in others.

Mont Brown and Pace-O Beats of The Astronauts drive through Southwest Philadelphia, anxious to start their tour of their old neighborhood—near 54th and Trinity streets, where much of the inspiration for their music is derived from.

They park a few blocks away from Mont's former home. As they walk down Trinity, Brown takes a moment to look down at the very spot where a friend was gunned down a few years back. He was targeted, Brown says, but no one really knows why.

Lyrics Reflect Violence

The Astronauts' music represents the truth of what they and others have experienced—it's sometimes violent and otherwise off-color, much like the way life was when they were growing up and still is for some of their friends today.

"I'm the one who does the lyrics," Brown says. "It's no hold punches. Everything I'm saying is real."

In his song "All I Had," the chorus rings: "I do this for my mom, I do this for my son/I do it with this rap or I do it with a gun/I sell a little crack just to eat a little lunch."

But The Astronauts also try to motivate people to do better. They took their group's name from Guion "Guy" Bluford, a West Philly native, who in 1983 was the first black astronaut to enter space.

"It's a message," Brown says. "It's 'Mona Lisa,' like a picture that is being painted. We're not lying, that's first and foremost. These are real situations. Everything we rap about is the God's honest truth. Nothing is fabricated. And I'm just telling these kids that Guy Bluford, he made it and we can make it just as well."

If you're glorifying it, I think people are just going to go with the flow.

Last summer, The Astronauts hosted a huge block party in Southwest Philly called the Stop The Violence Festival. With proceeds benefiting the Mothers in Charge Foundation, the intention was to bring the community together to show there are ways to interact peacefully.

"There was no violence the whole day," Brown says. "We just proved right there that we all can come together for one common goal and that's exactly what happened. I'm around this shit everyday, I know that we got so much potential to do better."

Brown continues the tour, coming to a friend's home, which is now abandoned. On the wall is a collection of old gum that is plastered to bricks, forming the words "54th and Ghetto."

It's the same rawness and bluntness of this mixed media graffiti that Pace says The Astronauts employ in their songs. A level of ratchetry grabs people's attention.

"It's quicker when you try to give a message, I mean, especially in our culture as black people," he says. "If you're glorifying it, I think people are just going to go with the flow."

And not hiding the ratchetry or debauchery of life from art, Mont adds, is actually a positive thing for his people, his community.

"I'm literally telling you what we're doing, you know, in the neighborhood that I'm from," he says. "The neighborhood respects me and him for doing this. No matter what I'm talking about, even though we're from the ghetto, it's still a positive thing that we're doing."

Violence vs. Voice

In our modern media-saturated world, where violence is regularly portrayed on television, in movies, in video games, in music and readily available anywhere on the Internet, the question of the impact of such messages is open for debate.

Music affects people. That cannot be denied. We would not listen to it if it didn't. But what are the lasting impressions that it leaves?

A 2006 study conducted by the Prevention Research Center at the Pacific Institute for Research Evaluation found that listening to rap and rock music positively predicted aggressive behavior.

Does violent, misogynistic or slanderous language make such ideas acceptable? Does it encourage us to live a certain lifestyle? Does it glorify the negatives of society?

Or, as Mont and Pace say, is music simply a direct representation of life, a relatively easy way for artists—and listeners—to have a voice in this world?

Do certain kinds of music make people commit certain acts of violence?

"Not necessarily," says Tim Whitaker, the executive director of Mighty Writers, a non-profit writing program for school children that received a grant to do a project about radio that catered toward blacks in Philadelphia between 1950 and 1979. "I think that's like taking something in a vacuum and pointing a finger at something more complicated than that."

Popular music always reflects the times that we live in, like it or not.

But music can influence the way a person thinks and feels, he says. He describes himself as being one of those white kids who listened to black radio when he was growing up. So much of the music being played on stations like WDAS and WHAT was being ignored by mainstream radio.

These stations gave a voice to a community that otherwise did not have many outlets anywhere else, and thus became a powerful vehicle. What Georgie Woods played over the airwaves became popular. What Mary Mason said was gospel. What Jocko Henderson did inspired.

There's been rapid change in the music industry, Whitaker notes, making it hard to see where the future of music is going. Record companies and commercial radio have lost their grip over popular culture, so the traditional ways of success in the music business don't work anymore. Today, artists can create YouTube videos and reach a level of fame that is unregulated by record companies or radio stations.

Popular music always reflects the times that we live in, like it or not, says promoter Sara Sherr, who has hosted the monthly women's rock series, Sugar Town, for 11 years. Artists can choose to rebel against conventional wisdom, she adds, with varying degrees of success.

"I think often the music is a reflection of their lives," Sherr says. "I don't think it's the sole cause of violence. Violence has always existed in our society. I don't think it was invented by rap videos, Marilyn Manson and Columbine, metal, etc., etc. Go back further and there's violent imagery in the blues and in murder ballads."

Violence Is the Same, Technology Is Different

The biggest difference between the music of today versus that of the past, Sherr says, is the technology that's readily available. It's now easier for people to make and produce music and to be heard.

Artists, producers and promoters in the thick of the current Philly hip-hop scene all have their own relationship with violence and music.

Hip-hop artist Jakk Frost says that his music is a reflection of what he might have gone through.

"I'm not in the rush for people to think I'm the realest rapper," he offers. "I have multiple messages. I don't think there is anything wrong with rappers making violent music for entertainment purposes. I'm not a one-dimensional rapper. I don't have no problem portraying myself as a ghetto superhero."

Frost says that artists should be left to their own devices, without having others dictate to them what should be said. The violence in the world isn't caused by music, he says. In Philly, the violence that gets discussed in music is rooted in the lack of educational opportunities, family structure and overall frustration about employment prospects, he adds.

"This is bigger than music," he says. "We let the cops discipline our kids. That fear of consequence is what's missing. It is affecting our youth to a certain degree. But art is always going to be a reflection of life."

Video producer Jay Wes says that the context in which violence and aggression is portrayed matters and it can also be interpreted differently.

Depending on what kind of person you are and what your surroundings are, it might seem offensive.

"It all depends on the people who are receiving the message," he says.

Wes, who makes videos for Philly talent like Suzann Christine, ICH Gang and Arsin, sometimes presents graphic scenes of murders, beatings and drug dealing. At times, there is an overarching message of stopping violence but at other times, it seems gratuitous.

"I always say there are certain messages for certain people," Wes says. "Depending on what kind of person you are and what your surroundings are, it might seem offensive."

Wes adds that even though some music may be negative, it can still make you think.

"Hip-hop is the only music where street credibility comes into question," he says. "R&B, pop, country? They don't care about that."

Wes says that if he were to go to any neighborhood in Philly and announce that he was making a hip-hop video and needed shouts from anybody, you would see most people shouting, "Murder Capitol" or "Killadephia."

"See, most of these guys are glorifying the violence," he says. "Yeah, I like it. I like hip-hop. But to keep it real, it comes down to the surroundings and the parents."

Promoter and Ruffhouse Records Vice President Jimmy DaSaint is an obvious supporter of hip-hop music, but does not support the negativity that is perpetuated in some music today.

"The music from the past was so much better," DaSaint says. "More meaningful, more creativity."

Music influences the youth in the way they speak, their attitudes and even fashion sense, DaSaint says. But music isn't the source of the ills of society. It's a reflection of them.

A person without a lot of social interaction . . . may rely upon music to learn social norms or to solve the problems within themselves.

A Violent City

"I can't blame a person shooting up a school on music," he says. "It's deeper than that. Philly is a violent city. It's filled with a lot of poor, uneducated people with no jobs and they think the only way out of the situation is with violence. You have to rob people to go get a better car or steal from people to get a better house. Poverty makes you do negative things."

DaSaint started promoting and working with artists before he was locked up in 2000 on drug dealing charges. When he was released in 2009, he turned his life around and is now successful in the music industry and as an urban novelist who writes about street and prison life.

"I just write what I know, and I know that life and that world because I was a part of it," he says. At Lucky 13 Pub in South Philadelphia, Chris Fear, one of the vocalists in wrestling-themed hardcore band Eat the Turnbuckle, mentions a recent Facebook conversation he had with a friend about a 13-year-old boy who killed his 5-year-old sister after practicing WWE-style wrestling moves on her. He elbowed, kicked and jumped on her, causing severe blunt force trauma, multiple internal injuries and internal bleeding. The boy later told detectives he knew the wrestling matches he watched on TV were "fake."

Made up of Philly hardcore all-stars, Eat The Turnbuckle puts on a wild show, with bottles smashed against heads, money stapled to band members and all six members covered in blood by the end of the show. It's violent and aggressive and real—there's definitely no ketchup or red syrup involved.

It feels good to get aggressive, Fear says, though he admits that there are audience members who sometimes take it to an unwanted level. But the number of people who go over-the-top is minimal compared to the number of fans who just like the music as an outlet.

"I feel like more often than not," he says, "the people who do something over-the-top are people who have mental issues because they are living vicariously through the music. If that music didn't exist, that person might not have experienced that because their imagination was not activated. Music makes you feel. Music activates feelings."

Music Can Form Identity

A person without a lot of social interaction, he continues, may rely upon music to learn social norms or to solve the problems within themselves. People like that are going to style themselves around music because they don't have an identity.

Despite their bloody stage show, Fear sees Eat The Turnbuckle more as raising awareness for wrestling and wrestling heroes. It's pure entertainment, not life coaching. Still, show attendees often get riled up and start throwing elbows in the pit.

"There is definitely a contingent of fans who want to get in on the action themselves," Fear says.

Eric Miller, editor of MAGNET magazine, says that most people want to listen to music that will support the mood that they're in. Music may resonate more because it's something you listen to over and over again, whereas not many people will watch a movie or TV show more than once.

But no matter what form of media they may intake, Miller says the responsibility for people's actions is ultimately on them.

"I think if you listen to a song or watch a movie and you go out and do something stupid, then you're sort of a dumbass," he says. "I mean, if you see a video that is violent and you go out and do something violent, I think more responsibility falls on you and not necessarily the person who's in that movie or who sang the song."

In a city with a very real crime problem, where the schools are under-funded and job prospects for young people can be grim, does portraying reality ultimately do more harm than good?

Music has been his salvation, Mont says. It keeps him sane.

Past or present, rock or hip-hop or blues or metal, can art depicting violence be considered fuel for the fire, or does it provide a much-needed outlet to rap, sing, paint or play, rather than do?

Back in the Southwest Philly, Mont talks about his father, Bucky Davis, who was a leader in the Junior Black Mafia, the powerful and violent drug dealing organization that ruled the streets in the late 1980s and early 1990s.

"He was a true hustler," Mont says. "So in that respect, yeah, definitely I am inspired by my father. I think I would take his heart and willingness to grind."

Mont doesn't know the exact story but says that his father was approached by a couple of guys who gunned him down. Davis was 22.

Mont now walks along Chester Avenue and points to the different shops, bars and restaurants where his father was known and respected.

"He used to run this whole strip," Mont says. "He was that guy, the Southwest King."

Many people in Southwest Philly now look up to The Astronauts, largely because The Astronauts took the initiative to do something. Where his father once reigned, people wave or nod to Mont, and a few people reach out to shake his hand or say hello. An elderly woman in front of an immaculate home asks about Mont and Pace's plans to build a park in the neighborhood.

Music has been his salvation, Mont says. It keeps him sane.

"There's a separation between Hollywood shit and documentary shit," he says. "We do a real life kind of music. That's what it is. Just the truth. I might talk to my friend. He might tell me about a situation that he might be going through with his baby mother or his job just fired him. I just try and talk about the real shit. No 'all these diamonds around my neck or new cars,' because that's fake. It's not for me. Here, ain't nobody doing that."

In Southwest, life is more humble.

"Niece need Pampers, my aunt got cancer/On top of that, Section 8 trying to take our house/Lookin' in the sky like God, what is this pain about?/Can't face our problems, so we take drugs to fade 'em out," Mont raps in "All I had." "Play the cards you was dealt because life is a gamble/Stand tall, fuck the law 'cause goin to jail don't scare you/Why would they fear you when death is right near you?/We're screaming our for help, but them crackers don't hear you."

Pace says that people in his neighborhood change their appearances depending upon what their favorite rapper is sporting at the time, and that kind of influence should come with responsibility. While The Astronauts are not at that mainstream level of success, they do have people who look up to them and try to emulate their actions.

"Even I need to take a step back from myself, from doing certain shit," he says. "That's the hard thing about being a rapper."

And when they rap about violence, Pace knows that the ultimate message of peace isn't always received.

"They want to take what you say out of context," he acknowledges. "But music is an art form."

5

Sexual Music Lyrics Harm Children

Penny Marshall

Penny Marshall is a writer for the Daily Mail *in the United Kingdom.*

Songs with explicit sexual lyrics are easily available on YouTube and iTunes, and middle-school and high-school-age children listen to them regularly in the United Kingdom. The sexual content encourages students to imitate the sexual language and causes both boys and girls to see girls as sexual objects unworthy of respect. Britain's laws around regulating sexual music content are focused mostly on television and are outdated when it comes to the Internet. New laws and new enforcement are needed to protect children from sexual material.

When Sally's mother learned her daughter was to be temporarily suspended from her church school, she was shattered. Her bright, bubbly, 12-year-old daughter had never been in trouble before.

Her mother, Jane, listened in horror as the teacher explained why. The school had discovered an obscene, pornographic poem Sally had written with a classmate—and then posted, naively, on the school intranet.

'Sally's teacher told me the poem was so disgusting she'd actually sent it to me in the post, because it was too awful to read aloud.

'She said it suggested such inappropriate sexual knowledge that the headmistress was considering calling in Social Services to investigate whether my daughter had been sexually abused. We were devastated.

'And when the letter arrived and I read it, I was mortified. The poem contained the most sexually explicit material I have ever seen. Even though I was upset, I could understand why the school reacted as it did.'

Sally had just copied what she sees and hears all around her; songs on the radio, music videos on TV and graphic, uncensored lyrics posted on easily accessible websites.

For Jane's daughter, who still went to sleep at night with an Enid Blyton book and her teddy, had written a poem which read like the graphic boast of a call girl.

But the subsequent school investigation uncovered that the poem wasn't a poem at all. It was, in fact, Sally's attempt to write a pop song, and every word had been inspired by the UK Top 40.

Sally had just copied what she sees and hears all around her; songs on the radio, music videos on TV and graphic, uncensored lyrics posted on easily accessible websites—which she can look at, without restrictions, at any time of day.

Sally told me she and her friends watch the music channels together in the evenings, on sleepovers to dance and sing to, and that they 'learn a lot of the rude stuff there.'

'We download stuff from the internet mostly, and from sites where we can send it free to our mobile phones,' she said. 'Sometimes we buy it from HMV. It's everywhere now—on our computers, phones, iPods. It's just not a big deal any more.'

But it is a big deal for her mother: 'As a parent, we thought we were pretty much switched on. I've got the internet covered with some parental controls. I've got the censors up and running on satellite TV—but I just didn't think about music: the online sites, the music channels. I thought it was all fairly innocent.'

But innocent this music is not. Today's lyrics are often totally explicit and so are many of the videos. Four-letter words are abundant and sex, quite often aggressive, multi-partner or sado-masochistic, is written about in body-part detail, and often more than hinted at on film.

This is a world away from the gentle hot pants of Pan's People or the sexy, suggestive lyrics of Marvin Gaye that I grew up with.

It is an ugly world where the songs celebrate drunken one-night stands and the videos often resemble porn. This is the world Sally and her friends are being exposed to and, in their innocence, trying to emulate at the age of 12.

Sally told me that one of the 'rude' songs that she and her friends have listened to, and which she copied, is called "Sex," by one of Britain's top hip-hop bands, NDubz, a North London trio of two boys and a girl. They've just won two awards at the Music of Black Origin awards (the MOBOs), for Best UK Act and Best Album, and have so far had three Top 40 hits.

Their album went straight into the charts at No 11 last year and has since gone platinum with sales of more than 300,000. They are increasingly popular with children, making an appearance on BBC's Children In Need this year (as non-singing guests). They were also special guests on the BBC Children's magazine show MTI, at teatime last month, singing their latest single.

'I like their music,' Sally told me. 'We all do at school. They've had three other Top 40 hits and so we thought their album would be cool. My friend bought it in the shops and "Sex" is on it.'

It contains these lines: 'I don't mean to be pushy pushy, I'm just in it for the p**sy p**sy./Do you ever get horny reading a text?'

There is no law to stop a child buying any explicit single or album from any High Street store.

The rest of the lyrics are too explicit to print in a newspaper.

Sally told me she was deeply ashamed when adults reacted as they did to her 'song.'

'My parents do tell me sex is a beautiful, private thing and important in a lasting relationship. But it doesn't seem like that with all this stuff about, and what I wrote didn't seem so bad when everyone else writes and talks like that, too. It's just a joke. But I got caught and made to feel dirty.'

The N-Dubz album is sold in record stores with a tiny parental advisory sticker on it (smaller than my little finger nail). This is part of a voluntary code for record companies. But there is no law to stop a child buying any explicit single or album from any High Street store. Retailers I spoke to said they 'used their discretion' when selling explicit items to children.

Yet on the website iTunes—where most children today buy music, because they can download it straight to their iPods—"Sex" (as a single) is on sale with no explicit warning, as is the album.

Sally had also been inspired by a song from Lily Allen. "It's Not Fair" is the lament of a girl whose boyfriend is no good in bed and who 'doesn't make her scream.' 'We really like that one, it's catchy,' she told me.

The refrain of that song describes the 'wet patch in the middle of the bed' which is left as a result of the girl performing an intimate sex act on her boyfriend. It was a massive Top

40 hit, reaching No 5 in the charts and staying in the Top 10 from February until June of this year.

Lily Allen sang the censored version of the hit on Ant and Dec's early evening Saturday Night Take Away in March and it is also played on the mainstream radio channels. It blanks out the offending lyrics, replacing them with a burst of the background instruments.

This song is popular even with primary school children. The trouble is, they don't usually listen to the censored version. It didn't take Sally and her friends long to find it on YouTube and iTunes and in the shops—and there's nothing to stop them, or their younger friends, buying it.

Sally told me she had also been influenced by pop videos, mixing into her 'poem' some phrases and ideas she'd gleaned from them.

Take "Hotel Room Service" by a band called Pitbull, which features a man inviting any woman he passes in the hotel corridor and lobby to come to his hotel room to take part in an orgy. Pitbull finishes up with three girls in his bed, singing about putting 'them fingers in your mouth, uh open up your blouse, and pull that g-string down south oooo!' This is No 21 in the Top 40.

Unless the Government takes steps to change the law, children such as Sally can continue to access videos such as N-Dubz's "Sex," which is verging on pornographic.

Another: Ironik's "Tiny Dancer," featuring Chipmunk and Elton John, takes a similar theme, with an orgy, naked women and sado-masochistic sex. This was in the charts for 27 weeks this year, reaching No 3.

Some say these songs and videos are doing more than influencing children to copy their lyrics. They are sexualising those who watch, changing profoundly what teenagers see as acceptable behaviour.

Dr Catherine White is the clinical director of the Centre for Sexual Assault Victims at St Mary's Hospital in Manchester. She is concerned that music videos are influencing sexual attacks via their sexualisation of young children.

She has said: 'I think it's all subconscious, and there's a drip, drip, drip effect. It might not be the one song, but all together it's having an effect on values. For the potential perpetrators, it's about knowing what's acceptable and what is not. And for the vulnerable people out there, it's about giving them the confidence to say "that's not right."'

Surely the Government, then, has a responsibility to protect the young and vulnerable from these music lyrics and videos? Shockingly, according to British law, it does not. While all the films we watch in the cinema are classified according to the 1984 Video Recording Act, which governs the age groups permitted to watch, buy or rent certain films, it does not cover music videos.

Sue Clarke, from the British Board of Film Classification, explains: 'At the time the Act was drawn up, no one imagined this sort of explicit material coming onto the horizon. Even if we do get complaints from the public—which we often do—we can't do anything about it.'

This means that unless the Government takes steps to change the law, children such as Sally can continue to access videos such as N-Dubz's "Sex," which is verging on pornographic. It would, of course, be remiss not to say that music channels on television, such as MTV, Kiss and TMF (available on Freeview), do abide by the 9 pm watershed—and don't transmit videos with offensive language or imagery before that time.

But, on the other hand, in today's multi-channel world, with more and more households signing up to broadband, the watershed is effectively redundant. Today's children access most of their music and music videos online, where there is no governance.

As part of this journey into the world of today's Top 40, I sat and watched TV's Chart Show with seven 12- to 16-year-old girls from some of London's leading day schools. I spoke to some boys separately afterwards.

The girls all loved the sugary Michael Buble and JLS hits which dominate the official chart show, and went some way to reassuring me that romance is not dead. But the girls told me it's not songs like those which appear to have the most influence on their age group.

'It's very hard for us,' one girl told me. 'There's a lot of stuff that's a spin-off from the Top 40 [in other words, ruder versions and other songs by the bands in the charts] which our parents don't even know about, because they never ask us what's on our iPods. It's a different world, and a lot of it is very dirty.'

Another 14-year-old girl said: 'I think it makes the boys behave differently when they are showing off in front of each other. They talk about sexual performance rather than friendship and use words like slut, whore and bitch to address us.'

One 14-year-old from a grammar school showed me the Facebook page of a friend of hers. It contained lyrics from another sexually explicit 'song.' This one was entitled "Sexy Bitch," inspired by a new track of the same name in the Top 40, featuring Akon. (It is played on the same radio stations and on music channels pre-watershed as "Sexy Chick.") A group of her so-called friends had got together and written a version of the song about her. They had then posted it on her website for all to see. Calling her a slag was the nicest thing they had to say. It was, I was told, 'a joke.'

It was also clear looking at the social networking sites that many teenage boys (and girls) are using sexual statements taken from songs to describe their 'status' on the site. One favourite seemed to be 'I wanna have sex right na na na'—

although the kids were not expressing themselves so politely. Preferring instead to use the F word. This line is from another Akon hit.

The boys were less open. One told me it was all about shocking the older generation and that was the only point of it. Another told me it was part of freedom of expression and sexual liberation. No harm done: 'Better to be open about it than not. Boys have always thought like this, now we're just straight about it.'

Jacqui Marsden is a psychologist who strongly believes that this copycat sexualisation is not meaningless.

'What's so bad about these videos, especially for young girls, is the message they give that women are primarily to be judged only as sex objects. They do not promote any other aspect of a relationship.'

And this is a tragic reflection on our society, because as long as the Top 40 remains so explicit and our children can access the graphic music and lyrics—without restrictions—we are squandering innocence in the name of adult entertainment.

6

Explicit Music Lyrics Can Raise Awareness of Sexual Violence

Jenny Valentish

Jenny Valentish is a journalist and author of the novel Cherry Bomb.

In the 1990s, musical performers like Fiona Apple and Courtney Love wrote songs that discussed sexual abuse openly and explicitly. Such songs are valuable because they acknowledge trauma and can help those who have had similar experiences. It is important not to censor songs about incest and sexual violence, because music can be an especially powerful and open way to deal with trauma for singers and listeners.

There's no doubt about it: we're better at acknowledging the sexual abuse of children these days. How could we not be, with blockbuster investigations against [American filmmaker] Woody Allen, [UK TV personality] Jimmy Savile, [Australian actor] Robert Hughes and [Australian musician] Rolf Harris turned into clickbait? But we talk about the topic in terms of disgraced celebrities, symbols of hope and dedicated days. We read about it either in news reports, or in op-eds cluttered with trigger warnings. All these conversations have their place, but where are the real, raw voices?

Back in the '90s, that's where.

Rock stars have long written songs about the imbalance of sexual power, but in the 1990s, with grunge and riot grrrl in full swing, we started to see a different take on the topic. Woman-at-end-of-tether angst became a trope, and songwriters were quick to take on taboos, with the sexual abuse of children being one.

Breaking the Silence: Ragers and Riot Grrrls

Fiona Apple, that thin, sombre girl at the piano, told the *Toronto Sun* that as a 12-year-old she was raped on the way home from school, which rose to the surface in 1994's 'Sullen Girl': "*They don't know I used to sail / The deep and tranquil sea / But he washed me ashore / And he took my pearl / And left an empty shell of me*". She told *Rolling Stone* that she became anorexic in an attempt to get rid of "the bait attached to my body". On self-harming, she added, "Courtney Love pulled me aside at a party and showed me her marks".

With '80s cockrockers banished to the dark ages, we were also witnessing the rise of the sensitive male. Front and centre was Pearl Jam's Eddie Vedder.

Love was herself influenced by the uncompromising Lydia Lunch, rolling promiscuity, shame, self-loathing and sexual power struggles into one spitball after another. If there's one character that's come to define Love's songs, it's the defiant dirty girl who takes the blame.

Love's former frenemy in early band Sugar Baby Doll, Kat Bjelland, went on to form Babes in Toyland. Bjelland wrote 'Won't Tell', sketching out only a vague impression with lines such as "*I won't ever tell on you*". She flipped the abused little victim image on its head with her 'kinderwhore' wardrobe of baby doll dresses and Mary Jane shoes, matching it with baleful looks and vengeful screams.

Similarly interested in subverting the idea of the victim was the original riot grrrl, Kathleen Hanna. In Bikini Kill's 1992 track 'Suck My Left One', she depicts a sister taking on the father coming into her room: *"We've got to show them we're worse than queer".*

Storytelling and the Sensitive Male

With '80s cockrockers banished to the dark ages, we were also witnessing the rise of the sensitive male. Front and centre was Pearl Jam's Eddie Vedder. His global hit 'Alive' tells the tale of sexual abuse by a mother and is one of a handful of songs on the theme; he was practically the patron saint of lost kids. Back in 1993, Eddie told an audience in Albuquerque that someone had told him if he ever wanted to heal from the abuse he himself had suffered, he was going to have to help others. I'd like to think he'd be able to write something catchy about the Royal Commission into Institutional Responses to Child Sexual Abuse—or the funds that the Abbott government has diverted from that into its own investigation into Labor's home insulation program. (And isn't 'Chaplains' already a Pearl Jam song? Probably.)

On a more fictional slant, in 1996, PJ Harvey released 'Taut', a short story about a young girl in the 1960s in her boyfriend's car that repeats phrases like a nervous tic: *"It was the first thing he ever owned, apart from me"* and *"I'm over it now".* Amy Grant also wrote about a fictional child abuse situation, in 1991's 'Ask Me'.

Liz Phair's 1993 track 'F*** and Run' caused a sensation upon its release for its fearless lyrics, which included the bravado-fuelled line *"F*** and run, even when I was 12".* It was recently analysed by a panel of women on *Popmatters.* Two years later, Jewel wrote 'Daddy' (*"I'm your creation, I'm your love, Daddy / Grew up to be and do all those sick things you said I'd do"*), partly about her own confusing childhood.

In the UK in 1994, Miki Berenyi from Lush was having a bold year, writing in detail about her molestation in the anthology *Women, Sex and Rock'n'Roll: In Their Own Words*. It was also coming to the surface in songs on Lush's new album, *Split*: 'Kiss Chase', for example, leaps between the shadowy memories of an eight-year-old and that child as a promiscuous adult.

The most prominent example of a current artist exploring the child sexual abuse issue is electro-grunge singer Sky Ferreira.

Also in the UK, Skunk Anansie's Skin wrote 'Charlie Big Potato' about the sexual abuse of a girl as her brother sleeps: "*I awake from blood thick dreams / Washing blame from my knees / Softly done, so secretly / I'm awake as Charlie sleeps*". That was 1999, the same year Anthony Keidis wrote the lyrics "*ning nang nong nong ning nang nong nong ning nang*".

The New Wave, and Why It Matters

And then it was like everyone was all confessed-out. In the noughties you had Kelly Clarkson, Pink and Christina Aguilera writing gustily about domestic violence and emotional abuse, and there was the Dresden Dolls' grotesque playground scene in 2008's 'Slide', but very little else. Until now.

In her 2012 memoir *Coal to Diamonds*, Gossip's Beth Ditto describes moving to Olympia as a teenager (birthplace of '90s riot grrrl) to inhale the remains of its fumes, after enduring a childhood of endless cycles of sexual abuse. Erika M Anderson, aka EMA, also made the pilgrimage to Olympia last year, hanging with K Records founder Calvin Johnson after becoming intrigued by the bygone scene. She wrote the intensely personal 'Marked'—"*Don't you know that I will never hurt you / You are such a pretty thing . . . I wish that every time he touched me left a mark*"—and told *Quietus*, "There are lots of forms of violence, and not all of them leave marks."

The most prominent example of a current artist exploring the child sexual abuse issue is electro-grunge singer Sky Ferreira. She hasn't escaped the description "nineties" in many reviews, and has revealed how much she was influenced by Fiona Apple and Courtney Love. She's also spoken in *The Guardian, Rookie* and *Time Out* about her own experiences of being molested. On her Facebook page she announced, "I've publicly spoken about [sexual abuse in my past] to hopefully help others."

Like Kat Bjelland of Babes in Toyland, who have just announced they're reforming, Sky toys with provocative imagery: the topless photograph of her looking traumatised in a shower, which became her album cover; the video to 'I Blame Myself', in which she's the waif-like runaway being handed over to a rival gang. It brings to mind Fiona Apple's child-sized body sprawling in lingerie in 'Criminal'.

"For the past few years, in mainstream pop, I feel like there aren't other people to relate to," Sky told *Time Out*. "I *knew* Fiona Apple. I knew what she was thinking."

And that's exactly why music is so important in tackling this most uncomfortable of subjects. Music doesn't exclude, intellectualise, stake ownership or try to define something. It's accessible to all and is a powerful acknowledgement of an issue—when sometimes acknowledgement is the most vital thing a kid needs. It allows the listener to engage with the subject or gloss over it, as is their preference. It also demystifies and destigmatises. There's no room for trigger warnings in rock music, unless that's just the name of the band.

7

Degrading Lyrics Don't Harm Women

Chelsea Fagan

Chelsea Fagan is a writer for Thought Catalog *and founder of the blog* The Financial Diet.

Robin Thicke's "Blurred Lines" music video, which shows naked women dancing, can be seen as empowering women by showing how men desire them and want them. Some women find the image of female beauty and power to be empowering, not degrading, and they should not be judged antifeminist or wrong for that. Everyone should be able to enjoy whatever music makes them feel happy without criticism or censure.

Earlier this week, I wrote an article about the song "Blurred Lines," and more specifically, how we should stop telling women what to be offended by—including songs like that. I (and other women I know) had been labeled "un-feminist" or expected to apologize for enjoying it, and I found the whole ordeal to be—if somewhat expected—extremely condescending.

Celebrating Women's Bodies

And while the response to that article was largely positive, I did receive several comments (both online and in real life) along the lines of, "But don't you know that song is so degrading to women?" And the truth is, I didn't. I had not noticed that that song—or the myriad other songs whose lyrics largely describe the sexual appeal of a woman and the sexual tension that is felt while dancing—was degrading. Because, at least to me, for something to be degrading requires a feeling of being actively degraded. These songs, beyond not upsetting me, actually make me feel quite positive as a whole. Perhaps they are degrading for some—and each person has that choice to make—but there is nothing about them that makes them universally negative for women.

If someone is happy shaking their tush in a club to "OMG" by Usher, good for them.

This past weekend, I was at a club with my best girlfriend. The music was good, we got some free drinks, and it was just one of those essential girls' nights that affirms friendship and the feeling of total liberation. At a certain point, "Sexy Bitch"—a song whose lyrics are undeniably as base and sexual as lyrics can be—came over the speakers, and we started grinding and laughing, completely unfazed by anyone who might have been around us. It was a moment in which I felt vibrant, and free, and wonderfully female. These songs, the ones we grow up dancing to, whose vulgar lyrics we barely even pay attention to, are an almost circus-like celebration of the hypnotic beauty of the female form. In that moment, so many of the girls on the dance floor were laughing and dancing together, feeling like the "sexy bitch" in the song and not finding it the least bit insulting.

In fact, I find these songs more amusing than anything else. The points of incoherence to which our sexuality and femininity can drive musicians and artists is simply astounding, and the songs which portray men as completely stupefied by the booty shaking in front of them, seem to reflect more poorly on the men for whom they speak than anything else.

To take the lyrics in this song, to own them completely and say to oneself as a woman, "Yes, we *are* sexy and appealing. You *do* wish you could be with us. And maybe, if you play your cards right and we decide we like you, we'll let it happen" is an experience that I and I believe many other women find incredibly empowering. When I hear 2 Chainz musing about how much he loves them strippers, I can't help but agree with his tastes. Seeing a woman completely in control of her body and her sexuality, dancing to songs that were meant to objectify her but only end up highlighting the power of her autonomy, is viscerally attractive.

Nothing Wrong with Enjoying a Song

Of course, not every woman is going to feel as I do. There are going to be women who hear "Back That Ass Up" and feel immediately repulsed or degraded. And that is completely understandable—not everyone has the same relationship to these words or these ideas. But that is a choice for every woman to make on her own, and there is nothing wrong with enjoying that song, or any other.

The important [thing] is that we all find what makes us feel happy and respected. And sneering at what might be part of that journey for another woman helps absolutely no one. Of course, part of the reason I feel that I am able to so thoroughly enjoy these songs is because I feel respected and affirmed by all of the relationships in my life—I never question my worth as a woman and as a human. I realize that this is a luxury, but it does not detract from the fact that the enjoyment of these songs can exist in tandem with a life that is fulfilling and intellectually satisfying. We can all discuss art, philosophy, business, and politics—only to get up and dance when "Pull Over (That Ass Too Fat)" comes on. While searching for respect and love is imperative for every woman (and every human), there is no rule which states where the feelings of joy and fulfillment can come from. If someone is happy shaking their tush in a club to "OMG" by Usher, *good for them.*

It would be unfair for me to uniformly label any of this music as "degrading," even if I find them to be on an in-dividual level.

If someone has made it their job, even, it is not our place to judge them—there are plenty of undesirable jobs in the world, and making money for being beautiful is far from one of them in the grand scheme of things. If a video girl or a model or stripper makes her living (and well) by dancing to songs that you perceive as degrading, you might be likely to tell her that it's a shame, or that she should be doing so much more with herself. But to all of the people who work in dangerous, extremely low-paid, menial jobs—who will never be respected or viewed as a truly useful part of society—we would never render moral judgments on their character. Video girls don't need your pity any more than construction workers or coal miners or late-night cashiers do. We are all getting by in this world, and doing it in a way that uses your skills and your advantages is *nothing* to sneeze at.

Taylor Swift vs. Robin Thicke

To be honest, there *are* songs that I personally find degrading as a woman. I am repulsed by The Beatles' number which starts off with the delightful lyrics "I'd rather see you dead, little girl, than to be with another man." My eyes roll out of my head and up through my sinuses when I hear yet another Taylor Swift oeuvre that portrays women as completely inca-pable of being the agents of their own destiny. I recoil on hearing acoustic numbers which so clearly rip into an indi-vidual relationship the musician lived through, which exists purely as a hatchet job to humiliate one's ex. All of these, to me, seem more damaging and more immediately insulting to our collective intelligence, but that is a matter of taste.

The point is that it would be unfair for me to uniformly label any of this music as "degrading," even if I find them to be on an individual level. If another young woman feels good and affirmed and happy listening to Taylor Swift, and finds nothing objectionable in the ideas it presents, it is not my job to slap the proverbial ice cream cone out of her hands. I'm not here to ruin her fun, and I'm not here to impose my taste level on her. Because to insult another woman for enjoying what she enjoys, or for being empowered by what feels good to her—for whatever reason—only serves to reinforce the idea that there is a "right" and "wrong" way for us to be.

Those of us in the corner dancing to Robin Thicke, laughing our heads off and feeling supremely feminine and awesome, we're doing just fine. You don't need to worry about this music hurting us or tricking us with its catchy beats. If we need your help, we'll let you know. Right now, the DJ is about to put on Ke$ha and we have some tables to dance on.

8

Criticism of Beyoncé Is Often Harmful to Black Women

Tamara Winfrey Harris

Tamara Winfrey Harris is senior editor at Racialicious *and is the author of* The Sisters Are Alright: Changing the Broken Narrative of Black Women in America.

Beyoncé is a singer who has been very successful, has controlled her own career, and has identified herself repeatedly as a feminist. Still, feminist writers often criticize her for her sexual performances and even for speaking positively about her husband. The criticism seems in part linked to Beyoncé's race, and the fact that black women are often seen as sexual or sexualized, whereas white women like Madonna can be seen as in control of their sexuality. The criticism of Beyoncé often makes her responsible for structural sexism she does not control, and it suggests to women that even the most successful and powerful are not good enough for feminism.

Who run the world?[1] If entertainment domination is the litmus test, then all hail Queen Bey. Beyoncé. She who, in the last few months [2013] alone, whipped her golden lacefront and shook her booty fiercely enough to zap the power in the Superdome (electrical relay device, bah!); produced, directed, and starred in *Life Is But a Dream*, HBO's most-watched documentary in nearly a decade; and launched the Mrs. Carter Show—the must-see concert of the summer.

1. This is a quote from one of Beyoncé's songs.

Is Beyoncé Feminist?

Beyoncé's success would seem to offer many reasons for feminists to cheer. The performer has enjoyed record-breaking career success and has taken control of a multimillion-dollar empire in a male-run industry, while being frank about gender inequities and the sacrifices required of women. She employs an all-woman band of ace musicians—the Sugar Mamas—that she formed to give girls more musical role models. And she speaks passionately about the power of female relationships.

> *The judgment of how Beyoncé expresses her womanhood is emblematic of the way women in the public eye are routinely picked apart.*

But some pundits are hesitant to award the singer feminist laurels. For instance, Anne Helen Petersen, writer for the blog Celebrity Gossip, Academic Style (and *Bitch* contributor), says, "What bothers me—what causes such profound ambivalence—is the way in which [Beyoncé has] been held up as an exemplar of female power and, by extension, become a de facto feminist icon. . . . Beyoncé is powerful. F*cking powerful. And that, in truth, is what concerns me."

Petersen says the singer's lyrical feminism swings between fantasy ("Run the World [Girls]") and "bemoaning and satirizing men's inability to commit to monogamous relationships" ("Single Ladies"). The writer also accuses Beyoncé of performing for the male gaze and admits, in comments to the post, to feeling "grossed out" by the "Mrs. Carter" tour name. And Petersen is surely not alone in her displeasure.

Policing Feminism

Turns out, booty shaking and stamping your husband's last name on a product of your own creativity makes a lot of folks question your feminist values. (Beyoncé recently told *Vogue*

UK that though the word "can be extreme . . . I guess I am a modern-day feminist. I believe in equality.") Some of the equivocation is no doubt caused by Beyoncé's slick, pop-princess brand. It is difficult to square the singer's mainstream packaging with subversion of conventional and sexist views of gender. But ultimately, the policing of feminist cred is the real moral contradiction. And the judgment of how Beyoncé expresses her womanhood is emblematic of the way women in the public eye are routinely picked apart—in particular, it's a demonstration of the conflicting pressures on black women and the complicated way our bodies and relationships are policed.

In a January 2013 *Guardian* article titled "Beyoncé: Being Photographed in Your Underwear Doesn't Help Feminism," writer Hadley Freeman blasts the singer for posing in the February issue of *GQ* "nearly naked in seven photos, including one on the cover in which she is wearing a pair of tiny knickers and a man's shirt so cropped that her breasts are visible."

A popular star willing to talk about gender inequity, as Beyoncé has, is depressingly rare.

Of course, in that very same issue of *GQ*, Beyoncé makes several statements about gender inequity—the sort not often showcased in men's magazines. Among them: "Let's face it, money gives men the power to run the show. It gives men the power to define value. They define what's sexy. And men define what's feminine. It's ridiculous."

That Beyoncé speaks the language of feminism so publicly is even more notable in a climate where high-profile mainstream female entertainers often explicitly reject the very word. Katy Perry, while accepting a Woman of the Year Award from *Billboard*, announced that she is not a feminist (but she believes in the "power of women"). And when asked by *The Daily Beast* if she is a feminist, Taylor Swift offered, "I don't really think about things as guys versus girls. I never have. I was raised by parents who brought me up to think if you work as hard as guys, you can go far in life."

A popular star willing to talk about gender inequity, as Beyoncé has, is depressingly rare. But Freeman insists flashes of underboob and feminist critique don't mix. Petersen concurs, calling the thigh-baring, lace-meets-leather outfit Beyoncé wore during her Super Bowl XLVII halftime show an "outfit that basically taught my lesson on the way that the male gaze objectifies and fetishizes the otherwise powerful female body." A commenter on *Jezebel* summed up the charge: "That's pretty much the Beyoncé contradiction right there. Lip service for female fans, fan service for the guys."

These appraisals are perplexing amid a wave of feminist ideology rooted in the idea that women own their bodies. It is the feminism of SlutWalk, the anti-rape movement that proclaims a skimpy skirt does not equal a desire for male attention or sexual availability. Why, then, are cultural critics like Freeman and Petersen convinced that when Beyoncé pops a leather-clad pelvis on stage, it is solely for the benefit of men? Why do others think her acknowledgment of how patriarchy influences our understanding of what's sexy is mere "lip service"?

Race and Feminism

Dr. Sarah Jackson, a race and media scholar at Boston's Northeastern University, says, "The idea that Beyoncé being sexy is only her performing for male viewers assumes that embracing sexuality isn't also for women." Jackson adds that the criticism also ignores "the limited choices available to women in the entertainment industry and the limited ways Beyoncé is allowed to express her sexuality, because of her gender and her race."

Her confounding mainstream persona, Jackson points out, is one key to the entertainer's success as a black artist. "You don't see black versions of Lady Gaga crossing over to the extent that Beyoncé has or reaching her levels of success. Black artists rarely have the same privilege of not conforming to dominant image expectations."

Solange, Beyoncé's sister, who has gone for a natural-haired, boho, less sexified approach to her music, remains a niche artist, as do Erykah Badu, Janelle Monáe, and Shingai Shoniwa of the Noisettes, like so many black female artists before them. Grace Jones, Joan Armatrading, Tracy Chapman, Meshell Ndegeocello—talented all, but quirky black girls, especially androgynous ones, don't sell pop music, perform at the Super Bowl, or get starring roles in Hollywood films.

Black women (and girls) have also historically battled the stereotype of innate and uncontrolled lasciviousness, which may explain why Beyoncé's sexuality is viewed differently from that of white artists like Madonna, who is lauded for performing in very similar ways.

Surely a woman can be powerful and simultaneously admit that her marriage is profound and life altering.

A *Seattle Times* review of a recent Madonna tour stop praises the artist for "rocking us as a feminist icon" and applauds the singer for her brazen sexuality: "stripping down to a bra, then pulling her pants down below a thong and baring her cheeks to the Key [Arena]." Even the *Guardian*'s Freeman, in an ode to *Like a Prayer*, the writer's favorite album, speaks longingly about Madonna's midriff-baring '80s fashion and the video to the title track, which "featured a woman named Madonna apparently giving a blow job to a black Jesus."

Through a career that has included crotch-grabbing, nudity, BDSM, Marilyn Monroe fetishizing, and a 1992 book devoted to sex, Madonna has been viewed as a feminist provocateur, pushing the boundaries of acceptable femininity. But Beyoncé's use of her body is criticized as thoughtless and without value beyond male titillation, providing a modern example of the age-old racist juxtaposition of animalistic black sexuality vs. controlled, intentional, and civilized white sexuality.

Feminism and Marriage

And then there's the fact that some cultural critics are adding to this dissection of Beyoncé's feminism through commentary on her relationship with husband Shawn Knowles-Carter, a.k.a. hip hop mogul Jay-Z. During an interview with Oprah Winfrey before the *Life Is But a Dream* premiere, Beyoncé spoke passionately about her partner of more than a decade, saying, "I would not be the woman I am if I did not go home to that man." This comment prompted Dodai Stewart at *Jezebel*, to write, "Wouldn't you like to believe she'd be amazing whether or not she went home to a man? (She would be.) It's a much better message when she talks about how powerful she is as a woman and what a woman can do—without mentioning Mr. Carter."

Surely a woman can be powerful and simultaneously admit that her marriage is profound and life altering. Beyoncé did not pronounce herself useless without marriage. On the contrary, she has said she was in no rush to marry the man she met at 18. "I feel like you have to get to know yourself, know what you want, spend some time by yourself and be proud of who you are before you can share that with someone else."

Being a feminist in the public eye should not require remaining aloof about relationships, including those with men who have helped shape who you are. We don't require this of men. None other than Bey and Jay's bestie, President Barack Obama, made a very similar claim about his spouse post-2008 election: "I would not be standing here tonight without the unyielding support of my best friend for the last 16 years . . . Michelle Obama."

Feminist media activist Jamia Wilson says, "I think that it's just hard for people to really grasp what it's like to be extremely powerful but also vulnerable. Black women, in particular, are characterized as singularly strong figures. How can you be the mule of the world for everybody, but also have somebody carry you when you need them to?"

If a woman loses feminist bona fides by becoming Mrs. So-and-So, someone best tell the 86 percent of American women who take their husbands' names at marriage.

More problematic to some is the name of Beyoncé's world tour—the Mrs. Carter Show. Jane Martinson of the *Guardian* wrote in a February 2013 op-ed, "There is almost something subversive about waiting until the strongest moment of your career, which is where Beyoncé finds herself now, to do away with the infamous glossy mononym in favour of a second name your own husband doesn't even use."

In a recent *Slate* article titled "Who Run the World? Husbands?" Aisha Harris wonders, "as a woman who has earned enough clout to inspire dance crazes, earn lucrative (if controversial) advertising deals, and perform for the U.S. president on multiple occasions, one can't help but wonder why she felt the need to evoke the name of her beau in her solo world tour."

If a woman loses feminist bona fides by becoming Mrs. So-and-So, someone best tell the 86 percent of American women who take their husbands' names at marriage. If there is any woman not in danger of being subsumed by a man's identity—no matter her last name—it is Beyoncé. In fact, the singer's married name is not "Mrs. Carter." She and her husband combined their names to create the hyphenate "Knowles-Carter."

"This man, who has made a living—an extremely good one—perpetuating hyper-masculinity, patriarchal masculinity, took the last name of the woman he married," Jackson says. "That in itself, to me, says something about gender in their relationship and the respect that exists there."

Beyoncé's race, once again, complicates the discussion. She is criticized for toying with the traditional "Mrs." moniker at a time of relentless public hand-wringing about black women being half as likely to marry as white women. ABC News actually convened a panel to weigh in on "Why Can't a Successful Black Woman Find a Man?" CNN has aired segments exploring whether the black church or single motherhood is to blame for rampant black female singleness. And men like comedian-turned-relationship guru Steve Harvey are making bank explaining to single black women what they surely must be doing wrong (see "Ill Advised," *Bitch* no. 56). And what they are doing wrong is understood to be not conforming to traditional ideas of femininity and not mothering in the "right" way (i.e., too often being unmarried "baby mamas" rather than married mommies).

Black women are, it seems, damned if we do and damned if we don't. Our collective singleness, independence, and unsanctioned mothering are an affront to mainstream womanhood. But a high-profile married black woman who uses her husband's name (if only for purposes of showbiz) or admits the influence her male partner has had on her life is an affront to feminism.

The conversation surrounding Beyoncé feels like assessing a prize thoroughbred rather than observing a human woman, and it is dismaying when so-called feminist discourse contributes to that.

Wilson says that in the context of pathologized black womanhood and black relationships, Beyoncé and the Knowles-Carter clan "counter a narrative about our families that has been defined by the media for too long about what our families must look like and how they're comprised." Black women's sexuality and our roles as mothers and partners have been treated as public issues as far back as slavery, even as family life for most citizens has been viewed as a private matter. Our nation's "peculiar institution" treated human beings—black human beings—as property. And so, black women's partnering—when and whom we partnered with and the offspring of those unions—were at the very foundation of the American economy. According to Jackson, "People would talk about black women's sexuality in polite company like they would talk about race horses foaling calves."

Beyoncé's Pregnancy

Like critiques of her sexed-up performances, response to Beyoncé's recent pregnancy illustrates that black female bodies remain fodder for public gossip. Even with the devotion of mainstream media (especially the entertainment and gossip genres) to monitoring female celebrities' sexuality, "baby bumps," and engagement rocks, the speculation about Beyoncé's womb stands apart as truly bizarre. Almost as soon as the singer revealed her pregnancy at the 2011 MTV Video Music Awards, there was conjecture—amplified by a televised interview in which the singer's dress folded "suspiciously" around her middle—that it was all a ruse to cover for the use of a surrogate.

The HBO documentary, which chronicled her pregnancy, failed to quiet the deliberation. Gawker writer Rich Juzwiak proclaimed, "Beyoncé has never been less convincing about the veracity of her pregnancy than she was in her own movie. . . . We never see a full, clear shot of Beyoncé's pregnant, swanlike body. Instead it's presented in pieces, owing to the limitations of her Mac webcam. When her body is shown in full, it's in grainy, black-and-white footage in which her face is shadowed." There is, in this assessment, a disturbing assumption of ownership over Beyoncé's body. Why won't this woman display her naked body on television to prove to the world that she carried a baby in her uterus?

The conversation surrounding Beyoncé feels like assessing a prize thoroughbred rather than observing a human woman, and it is dismaying when so-called feminist discourse contributes to that. Feminism is about challenging structural inequalities in society, but the criticism of Beyoncé as a feminist figure smacks of hating the player and ignoring the game, to twist an old phrase. "Beyoncé has no role in reinforcing or creating sexist structures," says Jackson. "Despite the privilege of celebrity, she is subject to the same limitations other women are. In some ways, she is constrained even more, because she has to always be conscious about her image. It seems odd to critique her instead of the larger structure that creates the boundaries and limitations under which she exists."

A tiny top and a traditional marriage should not be enough to strip a woman otherwise committed to gender equality of the feminist mantle.

Beyoncé exacts considerable control over her public image. (And she wrested that control from her own father.) *GQ* revealed that she has an on-staff videographer and photographer documenting most every move. The singer, or rather, her "people," famously requested that Buzzfeed remove some images from a slide show of the performer's "fiercest" Super Bowl moments. (It seems that the Queen was looking less than serene in a few shots.) Beyoncé's public life, from the reveal of her pregnancy to the first photos of daughter Blue Ivy's face, appears choreographed. And while many critics view that control as merely mercenary, it is well worth noting that this level of power is an achievement in an industry where "suits" retain significant control over "creatives." Beyoncé's attention to her image may well be her way of moving within the boundaries and limitations of gender and race that Jackson mentions. In *GQ*, Beyoncé noted, "I try to perfect myself." A quest for perfection may not result in raw realness, but it just might keep a sister on top in a society still plagued with biases.

The dogged criticism of the way Beyoncé chooses to live out her feminism must add to the pressure of being a famous woman of color. But celebrity brings with it scrutiny. More problematic is that many challenges to Beyoncé's status as a feminist role model make perfection the enemy of the good for all women concerned with equality, positioning feminism as nigh impossible to everyday women who can imagine being scrutinized for making the same choices Beyoncé has made.

Samhita Mukhopadhyay, executive editor of the popular blog Feministing, says, "[Beyoncé] is not allowed to be groundbreaking and traditional. She has to be Supermom or super hot stuff or super feminist. There isn't enough flexibility for her to just be who she is and for us to be able to say 'I'm not crazy about that decision, but this decision was amazing.'"

The Personal and Political

Juggling the personal with the political isn't easy in a biased society. We are, even the most diligent of us, influenced by gender, race, and other identities. And we make personal and professional decisions based on a variety of needs and pressures. Judging each other without acknowledging these influences is uncharitable at best and dishonest at worst. A tiny top and a traditional marriage should not be enough to strip a woman otherwise committed to gender equality of the feminist mantle. If we all had pundits assessing our actions against a feminist litmus test, I reckon not even Gloria Steinem and bell hooks would pass muster. Women must be allowed their humanity and complexity. Even self-proclaimed feminists. Even Queen Beys.

9

Sexism in "Bro Country" Is Harming Country Music

Amy McCarthy

Amy McCarthy is a freelance writer living in Dallas, Texas. She has written for the Observer, XOJane, *and other publications.*

Recent country music has been dominated by male performers. Referred to as "bro country," this music often depicts women in disrespectful ways and encourages men to ignore consent to try to sleep with women. The sexism in country is especially disheartening because in the past women country performers have been popular and have often been among the most innovative voices in the genre. Country needs to treat women with more respect and give more space to women performers.

In the past few years, it seems like everyone has been picking on country music. As the genre becomes more and more dominated by good ol' boys looking for a good time, the term "bro country" has increasingly been used by music critics to pejoratively describe some of the most popular artists in country music, like Brantley Gilbert, Luke Bryan and Lee Brice.

Country for Bros

Sadly, that descriptor doesn't miss the mark. Most of the charting artists in country music right now are largely men and the songs they write are targeted at other, mostly white and young, men. If you take a look at the *Billboard* country music charts right now, there are only two female artists in the top 10. Miranda Lambert's *Platinum* currently holds the No. 1 spot on the albums chart, along with an album from young TV star Lucy Hale.

But aside from the actual women in country who are making music, the subject matter of "bro country" is distinctly less friendly to women than the country music from the past.

It's already weird for grown men . . . to be calling the women that they want to have sex with "little girl," but the consequences are much more far-reaching than a little skeeziness.

Sure, George Strait, Conway Twitty and Garth Brooks sang about women and relationships, but the tone was much different. Classic tracks like "She Needs Someone To Hold Her" and "I Cross My Heart" have been replaced with "odes" to women that have much more misogynistic undertones, like Bryan's 2011 track "Country Girl (Shake It For Me)."

Misogyny in country music is a touchy subject. It has certainly existed since the inception of the genre, like every other style of music. Sometimes the misogyny is extremely overt. For many people, it's difficult to see why seemingly innocuous things like insisting on calling grown-ass women "girl" and reducing the subjects of these songs to pieces of their anatomy are a problem, especially when plenty of women are crowding into stadiums to swoon over their favorite country boys.

While these women are swooning over Gilbert and Bryan, female artists in the industry are being left behind. Last year, *Entertainment Weekly* actually asked Bryan what he thought about the difficulty that female artists were having breaking into the industry, and he attributed it to "girls" finding touring and early mornings too tough. Not to keep picking on

Bryan, but it's clear that he doesn't realize that he and his bro country buddies are a big part of the problem.

Let's start with the word "girl." Every genre of music uses this word to refer to women, but bro-country has a particular fondness for calling the young women that have caught their eye by "girl." Bryan alone has six songs in his discography that have "girl" in the title, all of which are infantilizing in their own right. It's already weird for grown men (Bryan is almost 38 years old) to be calling the women that they want to have sex with "little girl," but the consequences are much more far-reaching than a little skeeziness.

The same applies to the objectification of women in country music. We don't often hear about women as a whole in these songs, but we do hear a lot about their body parts. Entire songs are dedicated to "long, suntanned legs" and women's asses, and typically not in ways that would be considered empowering or even respectful. How can women sit at the top of country music when it won't even recognize them as people worthy of dignity and respect, much less as serious artists?

The women in country music have always been the ones moving this historically conservative genre forward as it kicked and screamed.

Country and Consent

Even worse, this trends toward a very murky definition of sexual consent in many of these tracks. In a time when rape culture is being discussed more than ever, the issue of consent in country music is being largely ignored. My brother, whom I often torture with country radio on our drives back to our parents' house a few hours from Dallas, astutely pointed out that a lot of these songs "sound like they're going to end up in a date rape." Even if they don't explicitly imply date rape, they sure do provide good background music for taking a woman out into the backwoods to try to talk her into having sex.

The theme is pretty simple. Take Florida Georgia Line's "Get Your Shine On," for example. The "girl" in the song is encouraged to keep drinking moonshine, then "slide that little sugar shaker over here" so that she can "rock all night long." Something tells me that Florida Georgia Line isn't talking about a guitar jam. Not to mention the fact that they're driving down what presumably is a country road, which doesn't exactly provide for many escape routes.

This kind of language creates an environment that's making it much more difficult for female country artists to succeed. In the last 10 years, only ten percent of No. 1 country hits were performed by women, a 14 percent drop from the 1990s. Bryan may think otherwise, but this decline likely has more to do with the ascension of bro country and the messages that come along with it than women being too weak to hack it on the country stage.

Country Women Past and Present

There has never been a shortage of talented, hard-working women making country music. Even in the beginning, though they had to scrape their way to the top, Kitty Wells, Loretta Lynn and Patsy Cline were some of the biggest stars of their eras. In the '90s, women like Shania Twain, Martina McBride and Faith Hill ruled the country airwaves, often out-selling and out-earning their male counterparts. More important, the women in country music have always been the ones moving this historically conservative genre forward as it kicked and screamed.

"The Pill," Loretta Lynn's historic homage to birth control in the 1970s, was a commercial success that did not come without controversy. Lynn's label refused to release the song when it was originally recorded, and country radio refused to play the song. Nonetheless, this feminist anthem helped propel Lynn into mainstream music and earned her a top-100 pop hit. Jeannie C. Reilly's "Harper Valley PTA," a tongue-in-cheek look at small-town slut-shaming, was less controversial but equally progressive.

With this history of strong women making waves in country music, it's disheartening to see bro country walking the genre backward. Making country music a better environment for women, both artists and fans, makes country music better as a whole. Talented female country artists like Miranda Lambert, Kacey Musgraves and even Taylor Swift deserve to have their music on the charts alongside artists that respect them as both women and musicians.

10

"Bro Country" Can Be Smart, Fun, and Harmless

Chuck Eddy

Chuck Eddy is a music critic and author of Rock and Roll Always Forgets: A Quarter Century of Music Criticism.

"Bro country" songs by male country radio artists are often dumb. But they can also be fun and inventive in their stupidity. Many songs cleverly reference earlier country hits and pick up hip-hop beats and themes from pop radio. Bro country can be sexist, but not more so than mainstream pop. Overall, the genre is often disappointing, but the criticism of it is excessive.

Sundry critics have deemed this an amazing era for country albums by smart women (Kacey Musgraves, Brandy Clark, Lee Ann Womack, Sunny Sweeney, all three Pistol Annies both together and in solo mode) but an awful time for country radio, which frequently tends to be dominated instead by brainless "bro" songs by pickup-flaunting, beer-swilling young men whose lyrics at best use women as racks to hang daisy dukes on. I more or less agree: My *Nashville Scene* poll top 10 last year was more female than ever, while the radio format's still pretty unbearable. That said, I like a few of the biggest and supposedly dumbest bro country hits anyway; I maybe even think they're smarter than they get credit for.

Dumb Fun

Zac Brown has famously called Luke Bryan's "That's My Kind of Night" the "worst song I ever heard," and he's not alone.

But Bryan's smash (No. 1 country, No. 15 pop) has a funk and push that Brown's own watered-down jam rock can't touch. Beyond signifiers about "rolling on 35s" and making it rain and T-Pain/Conway mixtapes and cornrows (as in hair?), the opening boom-bap beats and Dirty South crunk grunts and eventual internal semi-rhymes are evidence that, a decade after the first Big & Rich album, country has absorbed hip-hop to an extent that it's almost an unconscious part of the sound. This is neither a surprise nor as blasphemous as genre segregationists pretend—in fact, it's pretty much what country has *always* done with black pop music. And if the lyric's a sleazy come-on, it's no dumber about it than, say, "Get Lucky" or "Blurred Lines."

One last good thing about bro country is that it hasn't given up yet on trying to be John Cougar.

But admit it—dumb can be fun. And as any Ramones fan understands, self-knowledge helps. For my money, one of the most intentionally dumb hooks of recent times was in Lee Brice's No. 11 country/No. 62 pop "Parking Lot Party": "Ain't no party like the pre- [or 'freak,' if you want to hear it that way] party/ And after the party is the after-party." Redundancy FTW! Not sure I buy claims that Brice is bumping an R. Kelly groove, though I hope so. Either way, the song's rhythmic energy, goofball asides, drunken backup chatter and saliva-propelled "p"-pronunciation make for a funnier and more convincing approximation of double-shot '60s frat-rock than anything any so-called indie "garage band" has done in a while, even if this party's particulars involve chicken wings and tailgates rather than shing-a-lings and togas.

Brice tells us Marshall Tucker's on the radio, same band some bikini-top-popping lust object sang along to in Florida Georgia Line's country-chart-topping "Cruise," which took forever and a Nelly remix to make it to *Billboard*'s pop Top 5.

But neither song *sounds* like Marshall Tucker; if anything, "Cruise (Remix)" cruises along with windows down like Nelly's own old country grammar, maybe even in his old Range Rover. Word of Florida Georgia's onstage hip-hop medleys (Lil Troy to Macklemore to 50 Cent to Juvenile to Kanye) suggests untapped potential.

Hip-Hop Country

Personally though, I preferred Jason Aldean's far more ridiculous "1994" (No. 10 country, No. 52 pop), which is hip-hoppish in the sense that it's talked on-beat and references "The Real Slim Shady" and advocates imbibing Grey Goose á la the Ying Yang Twins. But it more endearingly rests on the dubious assumptions that (1) it's not too early to get nostalgic for the mid-'90s and (2) the main reason to be nostalgic is that we miss mulletted-and-mustachioed mid-level country lug Joe Diffie, eight of whose oldies get sneakily name-checked. His best, 1994's "Third Rock from the Sun," the only song about chaos theory's butterfly effect ever to scale the country chart, fortunately gets the most action; hence Aldean's truck turns into a time machine. Plus, the throb of "1994" is limber enough that, for its last minute, we get to bask in an instrumental jam. So stop complaining!

Finally, one last good thing about bro country is that it hasn't given up yet on trying to be John Cougar. So we got Randy Houser, who just a few years ago was positioning himself for the serious quasi-outlaw role Eric Church wound up in, now settling for the mere windows-down date fodder "Runnin' Outta Moonlight" (No. 3 country, No. 24 pop), salvaged mainly by that indelible "Jack & Diane" riff. Even better, last year gave us now-enlightened rogue Toby Keith's "Drinks After Work" (No. 28 country, No. 102 pop), which musically is straight-up *Lonesome Jubilee* Mellencamp and lyrically finds a casual sexiness in the after-quitting-time hump-day liaisons of middle-management office workers in "suits and skirts" sipping 7 and 7s. Suburban and mature, not "bro" at all really, but Toby's 53 and he's been-there-done-that and then some (was hick-hopping without making a big deal of it with "I Wanna Talk About Me" way back in 2001), plus he still sings all y'all young bucks under the floor mat. Enjoy your trucks while you can, boys.

11

Rap Lyrics Encourage Positive Capitalist Values

Steve Yates

Steve Yates is a writer for Prospect.

Hip-hop started out with a political, anticapitalist stance. Gradually, though, in America, and to some extent in Britain, rappers have moved toward an embrace of wealth, power, and entrepreneurship. Wealthy rappers have made fortunes and often have unprecedented control over their own business and art. Some criticize the focus on money and power as overly materialistic. However, for black people who are often stigmatized and disempowered, the focus on advancing through capitalism is ultimately a positive thing.

The latest album by the twin titans of hip hop has been a record-breaking success. On its release, Jay-Z and Kanye West's *Watch the Throne* had the highest ever first week sales on iTunes of any new album. A total of 290,000 copies were downloaded that week, and when CDs are taken into account, the album's sales approached the 450,000 mark. Hip hop is big business.

Watch The Throne is symbolic of the status that hip hop, or rap, has now reached. Originating in the South Bronx in New York City in the late 1970s, when performers began rapping over looped beats taken from soul and funk records, hip hop has since journeyed right into the heart of mainstream culture.

Rap Materialism

Jay-Z is married to Beyoncé Knowles, queen of R&B, and together they form the most influential power couple in global music. His wealth is estimated by *Forbes* at around $450m, and he has had 12 US number one albums (only the Beatles, with 19, have had more). Kanye West's fortune is around $70m. *Watch the Throne* is thick with references to wealth—even the sleeve is designed by Givenchy's Riccardo Tisci: "Luxury rap, the Hermés of verses," raps Kanye, giving the brand its French pronunciation, lest anyone should think he was mistaking the high-end goods manufacturer for a mythic Greek messenger.

The view of hip hop as a genre concerned only with the basest forms of materialism is a serious oversimplification.

But for its detractors, this materialism is one of rap's three deadly sins, along with its violence and misogyny. Casual fans of hip hop often see its materialistic side as something either to be played down or embraced "ironically." Some commentators judge it more harshly. When the riots broke out across Britain this summer [2011], many saw hip hop's celebration of materialism as one of the key causes. Paul Routledge, writing in the *Mirror*, summarised this view when he said, "I blame the pernicious culture of hatred around rap music, which glorifies violence and loathing of authority . . . [and] exalts trashy materialism."

Routledge is not *entirely* wrong. The story of hip hop's journey into the cultural mainstream is the story of its love affair with materialism, or, more accurately, capitalism. Its lead exponents, like Jay-Z and Kanye West, are brilliant entrepreneurs with vast fortunes (even if their music advocates a profligacy that is anathema to the savvy business operator). Hip hop's rise has been, at root, a straightforward process of free-market enterprise: an excellent product has been pushed with great skill and new markets opened up with real dynamism and flair.

Unsurprisingly, corporate brands have been keen to get involved. Darren Wright, creative director of the Nike account at advertising agency Wieden+Kennedy explains the appeal: "With hip hop you're buying more than music. It isn't a genre—it's a lifestyle, encompassing fashion, break dancing, the clothes or the jewels you wear. . . . The lifestyle is worth its weight in gold because it's not just about one rap song, it's so much more."

The view of hip hop as a genre concerned only with the basest forms of materialism is a serious oversimplification. It misunderstands the way that rap's relationship with capitalism has fed its creativity and led to both its commercial and artistic success.

Consciousness to Capitalism

While modern hip hop is unashamedly materialistic, its ancestors were different. As far back as the 1960s, artists such as *The Last Poets* and Gil Scott-Heron combined African-American music with spoken word poetry. But Scott-Heron, like others of that generation, was critical of the passive materialism that he saw working its way into black culture. As he intoned on "The Revolution Will Not Be Televised": "The revolution will not go better with Coke / The revolution will not fight the germs that may cause bad breath / The revolution will put you in the driver's seat." This political consciousness was taken up in the 1980s by the extraordinary Public Enemy, a New York group that mixed incendiary politics with apocalyptic music, militaristic dress and cartoon humour. Gentler, but still political, takes on "Afrocentricity" were advanced by the brilliant Native Tongues collective including groups like De La Soul, A Tribe Called Quest and the Jungle Brothers.

But by the early 1990s, this "conscious" streak was being eclipsed by the giddy thrills of gangsta rap. Its motivation was pithily summarised by NWA (Niggaz With Attitude), the group who named and codified the subgenre, on their track "Gangsta Gangsta"—"life ain't nothin' but bitches and money." Despite this apparent nihilism, NWA embraced the American dream with relish. They set down the unapologetic "money-is-all" credo of the low-level street hustler, in which drug dealing, guns and the police swirl about in a ferocious urban storm. Like other popular representations of American gangsterism—*The Godfather, Scarface*—it was a vision of unfettered free market enterprise.

While hip hop started off as an underground, and often political movement, it has for many years pursued an increasingly intimate relationship with business.

Slowly, the early political message was replaced by this focus on accumulation, both in the lyrics and also the business practice of those who were running the scene. One of hip hop's key entrepreneurs was Percy "Master P" Miller, who grew his No Limit empire from an LA record shop into a record label and then into a conglomerate. Miller spearheaded a new wave of hip-hop business by entering into joint ventures with music companies. He chose Priority, which was independent of the major record labels, and which had made a packet out of NWA and other leading artists. His deal brought all the benefits of working for major labels, such as distribution and marketing muscle, without the drawbacks—Master P was able to retain copyright control over the music and release records to his own schedule.

But not content with music, he diversified wildly: clothing, property, Master P dolls—even telephone sex lines. His debut film, the low-budget, straight-to-video *I'm Bout It* (1997) raked in sales that would have satisfied major studios. In 1998, Miller's companies grossed $160m.

In New York, the business interests of Sean "Puff Daddy" Combs developed along parallel lines: music, restaurants, a magazine, the inevitable clothing line, all name-stamped in a manner that led the consumer back to the man himself. Dan Charnas, in his masterful book *The Big Payback: The History Of The Business Of Hip-Hop*, describes Miller and Combs as "the embodiment of the superpowered artist, two one-man brands, the fulfilment of [the] vision of self-determination and ownership—not just for hip-hop artists, not just for black artists, but for all American artists." Having turned their art into business, they turned their business back into art. According to Charnas, their success "would mark the beginning of an unprecedented spike in black American entrepreneurship."

So while hip hop started off as an underground, and often political movement, it has for many years pursued an increasingly intimate relationship with business. Hip hop now has a materialist, acquisitive streak hard-wired into its identity. It is this embrace of capitalism that has taken hip hop from outsider status right to America's core. This ascent was neatly symbolised when Barack Obama, on the nomination campaign trail in 2008, dismissed criticisms from the Clinton camp by mimicking Jay-Z's famous "dirt off my shoulder" gesture. Asked which rappers were on his iPod, there was only one candidate.

Garage and Grime

British variants of rap music have been growing in success, too. Yet the contrast with America is marked. Maybe the conflicting attitudes are born of economic realism: the market is much smaller, and British hip hop has a limited international audience. That was perhaps why British rap's flirtation with outlandish "bling" materialism was comparatively short-lived.

In the early 2000s, the south London group So Solid Crew . . . emerged at the forefront of the "garage" scene. Its members imitated the flow, though not the accents, of American rap superstars over electronic dance rhythms that successfully merged influences ranging from American house and hip hop, to Jamaican dancehall and British drum 'n' bass. Instantly, they became the sound of young black London. "Proper [rap] songs started with So Solid," says Elijah Butterz, a 24-year-old DJ and label owner, over a pint of Guinness in a Walthamstow pub. "When they hit, *eeeeveryone* was into them. If you listened to garage you were cool. If you didn't you weren't."

If you're talking about popping champagne and then you go out on [the] road and you haven't got an amazing car and you don't look that great, then everyone knows you're a liar and your music's not real.

So Solid, along with other British garage acts, brought American-style bling culture to Britain's clubs. Smart dress, diamonds and champagne became dancefloor staples. But this quickly generated a backlash. Wretch 32 . . . is a 26-year-old from Tottenham who found fame this year with two number one singles and a top five album. He feels that the norms of American hip hop do not always translate well in Britain: "I think because of our culture, people don't go for stuff like that—someone making them feel like they're less of a person for having less money."

In response, east London rapidly developed its own sound, called grime—a rap-dominated genre with a harsh, electronic edge, and lyrics that sounded like a fight in a fried chicken shop. Chantelle Fiddy, 30, a journalist and label consultant, agrees: "Grime was the middle finger to [garage]. It was for those people who were either not old enough or didn't have the money to go to the [garage] raves. Someone like me, who came up through jungle and just danced like a dick in trainers, I never felt comfortable with garage."

Grime has had its triumphs. Dizzee Rascal scored a significant success with his 2003 debut *Boy In Da Corner*. Others, such as Tinchy Stryder, Tinie Tempah and now Wretch 32 have followed in Dizzee's wake, increasingly adapting the sound for the mainstream. But inflated claims of riches don't really fly. "In grime you can't really lie about it," says Sian Anderson, a 20-year-old writer, label consultant, PR and DJ for the influential radio station Rinse FM. "If you're talking about popping champagne and then you go out on [the] road and you haven't got an amazing car and you don't look that great, then everyone knows you're a liar and your music's not real, so you're back to square one."

Road rap is south London's counterpart to the east end's grime. Slower and meaner than grime, and with a closer resemblance to US gangsta rap, it's shown little interest in winning mainstream acceptability. Its biggest name, Giggs, has served time on weapons charges—he started in the music business when he got out. But his career has been dogged by police interference. His shows have frequently been cancelled and contract talks with a major record company were curtailed, reputedly after a call to the label from Operation Trident, the unit in the Metropolitan Police dealing with black-on-black gun crime. Then came Form 696, a risk-assessment form requiring London promoters to submit extensive details about themselves, their performers and even, in the original version, the probable ethnic make-up of the audience. After this, grime and road rap often struggled to get live bookings. Although the Met denied racial profiling, senior music industry figures complained to the Equality and Human Rights Commission about this stringent requirement.

Denied a live platform, they've found a new one online, notably on SB.TV, now confidently billed as Britain's biggest youth media channel. But not everyone cares about chasing the music mainstream anyway. "I don't want to be part of it," says Elijah Butterz. "Apart from Rinse, there's nothing there doing what I want to do. Everyone expects you to dig into the music industry, but as long as I can make money from bookings and merchandising, I'll continue doing what I'm doing." For Elijah, that means running the eponymous Butterz label, one of very few to still release vinyl records, DJing (for free) on Rinse and living off his DJ club bookings.

[British rap] is still a far cry from the US, where rappers get to hobnob with the president.

Endorsements

This quiet determination seems a long way from the hard-headed ambitions of American hip hop, whose outlook has always been more expansive. "There's no protocol to the things I'm selling because I'm selling my culture," Jay-Z's partner Damon Dash, told me in 2003. Dash was the driving force behind the growth of Roc-A-Fella, their jointly-owned music business, whose name is an explicit reference to the capitalist heights they sought to scale.

The relationship between American hip hop and leading brands has always been strong. Adidas sales spiked after Run-DMC's 1986 track "My Adidas"; Tommy Hilfiger went from obscurity to being the highest-traded clothing company on Wall Street in 1996 after steady name-dropping by hip-hop artists from 1992. Courvoisier reportedly received a 30 per cent sales boost in the US after Busta Rhymes released "Pass The Courvoisier"—the largest single rise since Napoleon III named it the official cognac of the imperial court. Its rival, Hennessy, the most popular brandy in hip hop, estimates that the majority of its customers are young black males.

British rappers are learning this lesson. Dizzee Rascal has had two Nike trainers of his own—an invaluable tie-in—and now owns his own label, Dirtee Stank. Tinie Tempah has a clothing range with Disturbing London, while Tinchy Stryder's Star In The Hood line looks a more durable bet than his records.

Empowerment

But this is still a far cry from the US, where rappers get to hobnob with the president. On *Watch The Throne*'s emblematic "Murder To Excellence," Kanye and Jay-Z contrast the black-on-black murder of American ghettoes with their lives of luxury. "Black tie, black Maybachs/Black excellence, opulence, decadence/Tuxes next to the President, I'm present," raps Jay-Z, before bemoaning how few black faces he sees at the pinnacle and calling on more to join him.

When critics zero in on hip hop's materialism, as they did this summer, they see just a fraction of the story—the fraction that talks about money, cars and glamour. But fixating on this element of hip hop ignores its limited appeal in Britain, where rappers have largely ditched the "bling" posturing of the early 2000s. When Wiley, the most influential man in grime after Dizzee Rascal, called his recent album *100% Publishing*, he was celebrating his bargaining power. It's a similar sentiment expressed by Margate rapper Mic Righteous, who, contrasting his homeless past with his present, raps, "I used to cherish every pound I got, now I cherish every pound I earn."

In the past 30-or-so years, hip hop has tried politics and it has tried gangsterism. But in the end it settled for capitalism, which energised it and brought it to a position of global dominance. American rappers like Puff Daddy and Master P, men who fought their way into the big time, did so by selling a vision of independence, empowerment and material success. That vision is also found, if less vividly, in Britain's rap music. And though hip hop retains unpleasant features, the core message, that people can have better lives, is incontestably a good one.

Organizations to Contact

The editors have compiled the following list of organizations concerned with the issues debated in this book. The descriptions are derived from materials provided by the organizations. All have publications or information available for interested readers. The list was compiled on the date of publication of the present volume; the information provided here may change. Be aware that many organizations take several weeks or longer to respond to inquiries, so allow as much time as possible.

American Family Association (AFA)
PO Drawer 2440, Tupelo, MS   38803
(662) 844-5036 • fax: (662) 842-7798
website: www.afa.net

Founded in 1977, The American Family Association (AFA) represents and stands for traditional family values, focusing primarily on the influence of television and other media on society. Though it does not support censorship, AFA advocates responsibility and accountability of the entertainment industry. The association believes that through its various products, the entertainment industry has played a major role in the decline of those values on which our country was founded and which keep a society and its families strong and healthy. AFA publishes a monthly newsletter and the *AFA Journal*. Its website includes articles on Christianity and popular culture.

Center for Media Literacy (CML)
23852 Pacific Coast Hwy., #472, Malibu, CA   90265
(310) 456-1225 • fax: (310) 456-0020
e-mail: cml@medialit.org
website: www.medialit.org

The Center for Media Literacy (CML) seeks to increase critical analysis of the media through its educational materials and related publications. CML was founded on the belief that media literacy is an essential skill in the twenty-first century as various forms of media become omnipresent in everyday life, and individuals should be empowered from a young age to make informed choices about the media they consume. *CONNECTIONS* is the official newsletter of the organization, with archival issues available online. Additional informative materials can be browsed by topic on the CML website, which includes several articles on media violence.

Culture Shock

2110 Hancock St., Suite 200, San Diego, CA   92110
(619) 299-2110
e-mail: angiebunch@cultureshockdance.org
website: www.cultureshockdance.org

Culture Shock is a network of nonprofit hip-hop dance companies dedicated to offering children and youth in diverse communities an alternative to street life by providing a rewarding activity and instilling confidence. Founded in 1993, Culture Shock has grown from its home location of San Diego, California, to cities across the United States, Canada, and the United Kingdom.

Electronic Frontier Foundation (EFF)

454 Shotwell St., San Francisco, CA   94110-1914
(415) 436-9333 • fax: (415) 436-9993
e-mail: information@eff.org
website: www.eff.org

The Electronic Frontier Foundation (EFF) is a grassroots legal advocacy nonprofit supported by member contributions. The organization specializes in cases in which they can help shape law in the areas of digital freedom, including more consumer-friendly file sharing rules. EFF's website offers a blog with the latest news of "the electronic frontier," as well as press releases and other information.

Freemuse

Jemtelandsgade 1, Copenhagen S   DK-2300
  Denmark
+45 33 32 10 27
e-mail: freemuse@freemuse.org
website: www.freemuse.org

Freemuse is an independent international organization advocating freedom of expression for musicians and composers worldwide. It is membership based, with its secretariat based in Copenhagen, Denmark, and was formed at the first World Conference on Music and Censorship held in Copenhagen in November 1998. It has published reports, books, and magazines on the topic of music censorship. These and other articles and news updates are available at its website.

Future of Music Coalition (FMC)

1615 L St. NW, #520, Washington, DC   20036
(202) 822-2051
e-mail: summit@futureofmusic.org
website: www.futureofmusic.org

The Future of Music Coalition (FMC) is a not-for-profit collaboration between members of the music, technology, public policy, and intellectual property law communities that seeks to bring together diverse voices to identify and find creative solutions to the new challenges of technology. FMC's website includes articles and research about music and the music industry. FMC also publishes *The FMC Newsletter.*

The Heritage Foundation

214 Massachusetts Ave. NE, Washington, DC   20002-4999
(202) 546-4400 • fax: (202) 546-8328
e-mail: info@heritage.org
website: www.heritage.org

The Heritage Foundation is a conservative public policy organization dedicated to individual liberty, free-market principles, and limited government. It advises parents to restrict the music and movies that children and youth consume. Its resident scholars publish position papers on a wide range of issues, including "A Culture Awash in Porn" and "The Culture War: A Five-Point Plan for Parents."

Hip Hop Association (H2A)
PO Box 1181, New York, NY 10035
(718) 682-2744 • fax: (866) 540-0384
e-mail: info@hiphopassociation.org
website: www.hiphopassociation.org

Founded in 2002, the Hip Hop Association (H2A) works to facilitate critical thinking and foster constructive social change and unity to instill tolerance, civic participation, social reform, and economic sustainability, while advancing hip-hop culture through innovative programming. H2A organizes an international film festival and publishes the monthly *Defuse News*, a news and information report that includes commentary, announcements, and resources such as grants, fellowships, and job opportunities.

National Center on Sexual Exploitation
1100 G St. NW, #1030, Washington, DC 20005
(202) 393-7245
e-mail: public@ncose.com
website: www.endsexualexploitation.org

The National Center on Sexual Exploitation (formerly Morality in Media) is an organization that opposes pornography by highlighting the links between pornography and sex trafficking, violence against women, child abuse, addiction, and more. Its website includes research on violence and media, including the report "Pornography as Trafficking" and "Adolescents' Exposure to a Sexualized Media Environment and Their Notions of Women as Sex Objects."

Recording Industry Association of America (RIAA)
1025 F St. NW, 10th Floor, Washington, DC 20004
(202) 775-0101
website: www.riaa.com

The Recording Industry Association of America (RIAA) is the trade group that represents the US recording industry. The organization protects the intellectual property rights of artists and is the official certification agency for gold, platinum, and multiplatinum sales awards. RIAA publishes the newsletter, *Fast Tracks*.

Bibliography

Books

Lorenzo Candelaria and Daniel Kingman	*American Music: A Panorama*, 5th ed. Stamford, CT: Cengage Learning, 2015.
Dan Chamas	*The Big Payback: The History of the Business of Hip-Hop.* New York: New American Library, 2011.
Laina Dawes	*What Are You Doing Here?: A Black Woman's Life and Liberation in Heavy Metal.* New York: Bazillion Points Books, 2012.
M. Gigi Durham	*The Lolita Effect: The Media Sexualization of Young Girls and What We Can Do About It.* New York: Overlook Press, 2008.
Tamara Winfrey Harris	*The Sisters Are Alright: Changing the Broken Narrative of Black Women in America.* Oakland, CA: Berrett-Koehler Publishers, 2015.
Murphy Henry	*Pretty Good for a Girl: Women in Bluegrass.* Urbana: University of Illinois Press, 2013.
Bruce Johnson and Martin Cloonan	*Dark Side of the Tune: Popular Music and Violence.* Burlington, VT: Ashgate Publishing Company, 2009.
Joe Kotaba et al.	*Understanding Society Through Popular Media.* New York: Routledge, 2013.

Marisa Meltzer — *Girl Power: The Nineties Revolution in Music.* New York: Faber and Faber, 2010.

Eric D. Nuzum — *Parental Advisory.* New York: HarperCollins, 2009.

Donald S. Passman — *All You Need to Know About the Music Business*, 9th ed. New York: Simon and Schuster, 2015.

Chris Rojek — *Pop Music, Pop Culture.* Cambridge, UK: Polity, 2011.

Tricia Rose — *The Hip Hop Wars: What We Talk About When We Talk About Hip Hop—And Why It Matters.* Philadelphia: Basic Books, 2008.

Paul Slade — *Unprepared to Die: America's Greatest Murder Ballads and the True Crime Stories That Inspired Them.* London: Soundcheck Books, 2015.

Bob Stanley — *Yeah! Yeah! Yeah!: The Story of Pop Music from Bill Haley to Beyoncé.* New York: W.W. Norton & Company, 2014.

Periodicals and Internet Sources

Robert Barnes — "Supreme Court Throws Out Conviction for Violent Facebook Postings," *Washington Post*, June 1, 2015.

Phillip Bump   "As Hip-Hop Became More Popular,
                      Crime Dropped. Thanks, Hip-Hop!,"
                      The Wire, January 7, 2014.
                      www.thewire.com.

Sarah Carson   "Why Sexist Country Music Is a
                      Turn Off," *Telegraph* (UK), March 7,
                      2015.

Jayne Dirt   "Is Hip Hop to Blame for Rampant
                      Consumerism Among Black Folks?,"
                      Clutch, February 2012.
                      www.clutchmagonline.com.

Lauren Duca   "Why Have Pop Stars Become So
                      Hyper-Sexualized?," *Huffington Post*,
                      November 10, 2014.
                      www.huffingtonpost.com.

Janell Hobson   "Beyonce's Fierce Feminism," *Ms.*,
                      March 7, 2015.

Derek Ide   "How Capitalism Underdeveloped
                      Hip Hop: A People's History of
                      Political Rap," The Hampton
                      Institute, June 4, 2013.
                      www.hamptoninstitution.org.

Independent   "Online Music to Get Content
                      Warning," June 2, 2011.

Anne Kiplinger   "Should You Censor the Music Your
                      Teenager Listens To? This Mom Says
                      No," *Chicago Now*, September 26,
                      2012. www.chicagonow.com.

Dahlia Lithwick   "Are You Threatening Me?," *Slate*,
                      June 1, 2015. www.slate.com.

John F. Mast and Francis T. McAndrew	"Violent Lyrics in Heavy Metal Music Can Increase Aggression in Males," *North American Journal of Psychology*, vol. 13, no. 1, 2011.
Amy McCarthy	"Country's 'Girl Crush' Controversy Shows That When the Bros Win, LGBT People and Women Lose," *Vice*, April 4, 2015. www.noisey.vice.com.
Erik Nielson and Michael Rendor	"Rap's Poetic (In)justice: Column," *USA Today*, December 1, 2014.
Elizabeth Plank	"A Feminist Takedown of Robin Thicke and Anyone Who Thinks There's Something 'Blurry' About Sexism," *Mic*, July 24, 2013. www.mic.com.
Jenn Selby	"Beyonce Pens Open Feminist Essay: 'We Need to Stop Buying Into the Myth of Gender Equality,'" *Independent*, July 1, 2015.
Jordan Silver	"In Defence of Robin Thicke's 'Blurred Lines' Through the Work of Manet, Duchamp, and Ratajowski," *Vice*, September 10, 2013. www.noisey.vice.com.
Cherise Smith	"Why I'm Not Buying Beyoncé's Brand of Feminism," *Womansenews*, October 17, 2014. www.womansenews.com.

Emily Sohn   "Song Lyrics Getting Sexier. Should
                     We Care?," *Discovery*, September 15,
                     2011. www.news.discovery.com.

William West   "Families Becoming Own Censors,"
                     Mercatornet, September 17, 2009.
                     www.mercatornet.com.

Carl Wilson   "The Problem with Country for
                     People Who Don't Like Country,"
                     Slate, June 26, 2015. www.slate.com.

Index

CPSIA information can be obtained
at www.ICGtesting.com
Printed in the USA
FFOW05n0230160116